Understanding the
Former Prisoner of War

Life After Liberation

Essays by Guy J. Kelnhofer Jr., Ph.D.

Former Prisoner of War, Wake Island, 1941-1945

edited by Amy Lindgren

Banfil Street Press, St. Paul, Minnesota

Published by
Banfil Street Press
244 Banfil Street
St. Paul, Minnesota 55102

First Printing June, 1992
Printed in the United States of America

ISBN 0-9633008-0-6
ISBN 0-9633008-1-4 paperback
Library of Congress Catalog Card Number 92-81598

Cover design and page layout by Betsy Scholl, Scholl Design, St. Paul, Minnesota.

Several essays printed here were first published in magazines and newspapers including *Ex-POW Bulletin, The Little WigWag, St. Paul Pioneer Press, Stars and Stripes, Quan*. An early version of "Questioning Japan's Honor" is also entered in the Congressional Record (March 21, 1990).

From too much love of living,
  From hope and fear set free,
We thank with brief thanksgiving
  Whatever gods may be

That no life lives forever;
That dead men rise up never;
That even the weariest river
  Winds somewhere safe to sea.

Algernon Charles Swinburne,
"The Garden of Proserpine"

Contents

Foreword

In publishing these essays on the lives of prisoners of war after liberation, Dr. Kelnhofer has shown the quality of courage which sustained him through more than three and a half years of captivity. Other books have been written about the POW experience — the physical abuse and cruelty endured, the loss of so many buddies, the bravery of the men, their coping and surviving mechanisms, and the sabotage and resistance. These are graphic accounts of horror-filled events, but they do not deal with the ways the men were affected for the rest of their lives. It is difficult for any person to bare his soul and reveal his emotional distress publicly; for an ex-POW to whom emotion is dangerous, it takes extraordinary bravery. As Guy tells what life has been like for him and his wife Maria for the past 40 years, thousands of other ex-POWs and their families learn that we are not alone in dealing with the difficult-to-diagnose physical diseases, the misunderstanding by public and professionals, and the depression, anxiety and other emotional problems that beset us. It helps to learn that the roots of these troubles lie in the captivity experience and are shared to some degree by all ex-POWs.

A significant number of American service men and women became enemy captives during World War II. The prisoners in Asia, of whom Dr. Kelnhofer writes, were treated especially cruelly since the Japanese made no pretense of adhering to the Geneva Convention on the treatment of prisoners. More than one-third died in captivity. The rest were starved, tortured, terrorized and degraded. Unwittingly they became 'de facto' subjects in an experiment on human reaction to extreme brutality and total loss of control over one's destiny. When the survivors returned home in 1945, little thought was given to the long-term effects of their captivity. Many were told that a good diet and reunion with their families would quickly restore them to normal. We now recognize how naive this was. As Dr. Kelnhofer documents, in spite of all efforts to put the past behind, it was impossible to overcome the extreme physical and emotional damage done.

After 30 or more years of unexplained suffering, Dr. Kelnhofer and other ex-POWs began to speak out and a body of knowledge started to develop about the profound residual effects of the POW experience. It was at about this time at an American Ex-POW meeting that my husband and I first met Guy and Maria. We learned from and developed a deep respect for them, shared experiences, and became friends. In the late 1970s and early 80s, some Veterans Administration offices around the country began special outreach programs for ex-POWs and their families. We benefited from the heightened awareness of the men's unusual medical problems and from the supportive discussion groups, although these in no way made up for 30 years of failure to understand and treat. The majority of World War II ex-POWs have not had even this belated help, and with advancing age they are suffering even more acutely from their war-related disabilities. Current budget cutting and preoccupation with other issues indicates that the VA, in spite of existing legislation, is again pushing World War II men into the background. This is unjust, for these men have served doubly, first in the war and then as instructional models. On the basis of knowledge gained from Guy and others, the ex-POWs from Vietnam were treated more promptly and extensively, while our currently returning hostages are met by batteries of medical and psychiatric professionals. We are glad that the knowledge gained from World War II ex-POWs is being used to help others, but surely this pioneer group also deserves to receive the best available treatment and compensation for their suffering.

Guy Kelnhofer's book is especially timely now. To the ex-POWs and their families he offers important information, self-respect, deep insights, and strength. To the professionals, especially VA personnel, this book is a window into the minds and bodies of former prisoners of war. Understanding this material should greatly enhance the treatment of ex-POWs. The book is a powerful reminder to the country and the government of the horrors that result from wars and of the debt that we owe to those who endured them to defend us.

Rachel Nelson
Wife of Gordon Nelson, prisoner of the Japanese, 1942-45

Preface

The material in this publication is a collection of separate articles, nearly all of them published in newspapers and magazines over the past few years. The purpose in assembling them here is to make them more accessible to the select audiences for which they were written: the former prisoners of war and their families, and the Department of Veterans Affairs (DVA). My motivation for writing these essays is to help all of those who are involved with former prisoners of war to understand how deeply the imprisonment experience has affected these veterans. It has also been an exercise in learning for me. Through my work on these essays I have gained a better understanding of my own behavior as a former prisoner of war.

Most of us who were held captive in the more brutal prison camps have coped with the aftereffects of that experience by a process of denial. For 40 years, I was careful to avoid any and all reminders of that terrible time. It was only a few years ago that I began to associate with my former prison camp comrades. But those of us who belong to organizations of former prisoners and who actively participate in their activities are only a small proportion of the total number of prison camp survivors. I believe that the majority of these disabled veterans do not understand the extent to which they have been affected by their imprisonment experiences. They cope, as I once did, by repressing and denying that painful past history.

Much of what I have written here concerns the mental health and the behavior of former prisoners of war. It is appropriate to question my authority for expressing these opinions, as my field of expertise is river basin planning, not mental health. What gives me the right and the obligation to speak out is my own background as a former prisoner of the Japanese, and my recent efforts to understand the effects of that imprisonment. For several years now, I have been attending ex-POW therapy groups organized by the DVA. Here former prisoners of war gather to discuss the stresses of coping with daily living. While not every ex-POW can be convinced to attend these groups, I have found the benefits immeasurable. Indeed, it was participation in group therapy that first spurred me to re-examine my own experiences and eventually resulted in these essays. Exchanging views with others of a similar experiential background has taught me much, and I feel an obligation to share this information with others who need to know. In the essay "Group Therapy and the Ex-POW" I discuss these sessions and the benefits they offer.

Despite the DVA's sponsorship of these therapy groups, it has been my experience and that of many of my fellows that the Department is not very well informed about the effects that imprisonment has had on this group of disabled veterans. As a consequence, relatively few former prisoners of war receive appropriate compensation for those service related injuries that originated during their captivity. Monetary compensation for their war-related disabilities would be welcomed by all of these deserving veterans. However, for most, it is likely that the money itself is not the real issue. The denial of compensation awards by the DVA represents to these disabled veterans a belittling by their government of the great personal sacrifices they and their families have made, and continue to make, as a result of their service. A number of the following essays deal with the issue of unrecognized service, and the anger justly felt by the former prisoner of war. The essay entitled "Disability Rating Problems for Ex-POWs" details specific problems in the processes used by the DVA and offers suggestions to rectify them.

Few in the public or in the government are aware of the damages suffered by the wives and children as a result of living intimately with these survivors. In fact, it is unusual for a former prisoner of war to have any appreciation of how his prison camp experiences impinge on the health and welfare of his family. My wife, Maria, who is a physician specializing in mental health, educated me and many others to this aftereffect of imprisonment. Through her speeches and writings, she has made a valuable contribution to our understanding of this hidden, secondary damage. Some of her previously published remarks are included here for the broader picture they present of the ex-POW as husband and father.

No attempt has been made to describe here the experiences of all former prisoners of war. Because the essays are based on my own experiences, and those of my comrades, the point of reference is to male survivors of Japanese prison camps in World War II. Nevertheless, the long-term effects of living in brutal, unjust captivity are universal to that experience. Survivors of other prison camps, political hostages and even victims of long-term domestic abuse will recognize in these essays their own responses and survival mechanisms. What we have in common is that we lost all control over our daily lives, lived in constant fear of sudden death, were isolated from the world we had known and were treated with extreme cruelty by our captors.

It is true that some prisoners of war were held for relatively short periods. Some were well-treated during their incarceration, and some even had cause to be glad that they had been taken captive. These lucky few are not considered in my accounts of the aftereffects of the prisoner of war experience. Rather, my remarks are addressed to those many thousands of former prisoners of war who were so traumatized by what they endured that they suffered the effects for the remainder of their lives, and to their families, who stood by in support and love, even when they found no support themselves.

One of the essays included in this collection, "Questioning Japan's Honor", may be seen by some as a more political piece. It is not popular today to hold Japan responsible for the unexpected destruction and slaughter at Pearl Harbor and for the ensuing war with America. But, for the survivors of Japan's prison camps, there will be no real healing until that nation recognizes and apologizes for its aggression and its terrible brutality. The anger of POW survivors toward Japan is not racism, as has been sometimes charged. Rather, it is an honest and just response to the unacknowledged brutality suffered at the hands of Japanese captors. Forgiveness is an essential part of the readjustment process for former prisoners of war. How can the angry, wounded survivors even consider forgiveness when their captors refuse to admit that they deliberately killed and maltreated those captured servicemen?

* * *

This has been a difficult project for me, culminating years of research and personal reflection. Because of my own emotional limitations, I found myself unable to put these writings together in a single format. I was fortunate to enlist the help of Amy Lindgren, a freelance writer, who is also an old family friend. She has used her editorial skills and her considerable personal empathy to do what I have not been able to do in assembling and editing these writings. There is no doubt that she has made this otherwise impossible project possible. I am grateful for her contribution.

Many comrades in arms have confided in me and have helped me to obtain a deeper understanding of the commonalities of our prison camp experiences and of their effects on our daily lives. The unhappy circumstances of these comrades and their families have provided my principal motivation in bringing to light our fates since liberation. None of these brave men and women are responsible for the judgments I have made nor for the conclusions I have drawn. Any errors here are of my own making.

My special thanks to my wife, Maria Kelnhofer, M.D., for her loyal support, unwavering love and constant encouragement. Without her, I know that this and every other endeavor of mine would have been impossible.

Acknowledgements

The author and editor gratefully acknowledge the assistance of countless people in the preparation of this book, as well as organizations such as the Veterans Administration, the War Amputations of Canada, and membership groups representing the former prisoner of war.

We would like to express our gratitude to these contributors:

Rachel and Gordon Nelson, Irving Silverlieb, John Whipple, Harold Kurvers, Anne Massey, Charles Williams, Wallace Carroll, Ward Gardner, Geraldine Meek, Otis Jones, Ann Franklin, Leona Dye, Charles and Tula Brown, the late Dr. Leslie Caplan, and Robert Larson, who entertained us with his stories of wartime exploits, but died before he could see this book in print.

Several people also provided technical assistance and support, including Harold and Virginia Page, Colonel Arthur Poindexter, Elmer Long, Gregory Urwin, Floyd Nagler, Brian Engdahl, Raina Eberly and Dr. William Shadish.

In addition, we'd like to acknowledge Charles Stenger and Stan Sommers, whose work on behalf of former POWs has laid the foundation for books like this one.

It is a continuing effort to alert the world to the injustices suffered by former prisoners of war. We thank everyone who works toward that understanding.

Introduction

Starvation, beatings, torture, brainwashing, slavery, vivisection, even cannibalism. Reading the transcripts from war trials over the years, it would seem there is no treatment too cruel or inhuman to apply to a prisoner of war. And these have not been isolated incidents, practiced on a few hapless soldiers caught behind enemy lines. One of the shocking secrets about prisoners of war is the sheer numbers involved. In World War II alone, an estimated 35 million civilians and soldiers were held captive by the various powers. *35 million!* Of the 15 million who were soldiers, between six and 10 million perished or simply disappeared. Of the Allied forces, over a quarter-million were held by the Germans; another 95,000 were captured by the Japanese. And more than a third of the soldiers taken by the Japanese died in the camps, most often from disease, starvation, or murder.

What does it mean to be a prisoner of war, to have lived through those experiences? What happens to the human soul, the psyche, the mind during prolonged periods of starvation and brutality? What happens later, when the soldier is liberated, examined and summarily released back into society, all in the same few weeks, with no thought to continued care or follow-up?

And what about the former POW's family: are there no residual effects of living with an ex-POW?

Of the 142,000 American soldiers known to have been held captive by enemy forces in this century, approximately 68,000 are alive today. Nearly all of them are World War II veterans, now in their retirement years.

What has become of them? How have they lived? What effect have their captivity experiences had on their lives and on their families?

We don't know. In fact, we know surprisingly little of the men and women who gave more than their lives in the service of America. Few studies have been commissioned, few articles written about their lives back home. In particular, we know little about their health, and the repercussions on the human body of starvation, disease, and injury left untreated over long periods of time.

What we do know comes from the survivors themselves. Dr. Guy Kelnhofer, Jr., the author of these essays, has spent a lifetime examining the POW experience. Held for nearly four years by the Japanese, Dr. Kelnhofer was little more than 24 when he gained his freedom at the end of World War II. During his imprisonment, he saw friends tortured and murdered, enslaved as coal miners, stevedores, shipyard and steel mill hands, and starved until they could no longer lift themselves from the mud.

Dr. Kelnhofer was one of the lucky ones – a survivor. But what kind of existence has it been? Characterized by bouts of depression, alcohol abuse, constant moves, and job transfers, Dr. Kelnhofer's life has been a patchwork of coping with past demons. Now retired with a 100% disability rating, Dr. Kelnhofer still awakens from nightmares, more than 45 years after his release. Attacks of vertigo come on suddenly and leave just as quickly, and his hearing is all but destroyed.

And yet he's lucky, because he knows what's happening to him. So many former POWs live in a world of silence, unable to tell others about their experience. Some have never told their spouses. Inherent in the POW psyche is a profound sense of shame and guilt for being captured, even when there was no possible escape.

There is also survivor guilt to contend with, along with the memory of buddies who didn't make it, rage at their captors, and the long-term effects of a lifetime of psychic numbing. None of these feelings diminishes over the years. Indeed, they intensify, creating a profound loss of power and self-esteem. Unexpressed, they can wreak havoc by coming out in insidious ways – chemical dependency, spouse battering and child abuse, even severe self-neglect and suicide.

In this book of essays, Dr. Kelnhofer charts the effects of imprisonment on former POWs, using his own life as a model. His wife Maria adds her voice, representing the issues of spouses and families.

This has not been an easy task, and Dr. Kelnhofer is to be commended for his courage and honesty in pursuing it. In the decade since he began writing about these issues, he has become a beacon for other ex-POWs and their families, many of whom believed they were alone in their experiences. Excerpts from their letters to both Guy and Maria are printed in the margins of the text. Their words attest to the need for this book and for the changes Dr. Kelnhofer advocates in this nation's treatment of ex-POWs.

Here's hoping those changes come about in time to benefit surviving ex-POWs. May theirs be the last generation to suffer as they have.

Amy Lindgren

Santo Tomas prison camp internees Lee Rogers and John Todd. Courtesy of American ExPrisoners of War, Inc.

Ex-Prisoners of War: Fact or Fiction?

In March 1991, an end was called to the Persian Gulf War, fewer than six weeks after it started. That war resulted in 23 American prisoners of war, most taken in the last month of fighting. On March 9, all the POWs were returned to their countries, amid widespread celebration and media attention. American POWs were greeted by President Bush and his wife, and honored as heroes by school children. Could there be any doubt of their sacrifice, and America's gratitude?

And yet, their story is not typical of the national response to former POWs as a group. Perhaps because there were so few, or because the war was so short, these 23 received more attention in a day than POW survivors of previous conflicts normally receive in a lifetime. In general, former POWs are the forgotten veterans, overlooked in everything from medical studies to disability ratings. Even in veterans facilities, very little is known about the special needs of someone who has been starved, beaten, worked to exhaustion and routinely exposed to life-threatening disease for periods of years.

Indeed, few military prisoners of war ever receive special recognition for the sufferings they have endured. When World War II came to an end, thousands of American servicemen were released from prison camps in Europe, Africa, and Asia. Although many had been imprisoned for years under inhuman conditions, they returned largely unnoticed among the large mass of troops demobilized at war's end.

On April 9, 1987, more than 40 years after the end of World War II, President Reagan proclaimed a National POW Remembrance Day. Even such a small tribute was not without its critics. Some wondered why former prisoners of war should merit a national day of their own. What is there about being a prisoner of war to justify remembrance by the American people?

Fighters or Quitters?

Despite the enthusiastic media coverage of the Persian Gulf War, it is my belief that a number of people today look upon former prisoners of war with distrust and even disdain. At the least, their views are founded in ignorance. Examples abound: when Congress authorized a special medal award for former prisoners of war in 1987, the dissenters included a man who wrote to the editor of a military magazine protesting that the medals should be reserved for those who fought, not those who surrendered.[1]

"Sometimes, Guy, strange images molest my thoughts, memories of no real significance, yet intense, like charged particles in a science fiction dream. Memories . . . trances, it's hard to say what they are. It's as if I slip out of time, as if the past and the present have collapsed into one unbroken instant, so that I'm both myself, and myself at nineteen, the age when I was squatting in a bomb crater on Corregidor, roasting monkey meat with Truax and Havel (both dead), wondering when the promised relief would come and if we'd be alive when it did. And we waited and waited, but no one came. Promises, promises ..."

> *Robert V. Larson*
> *Plymouth, Minnesota*
> *(from the unpublished novel,* The Color of Ashes*)*

A friend who checked into a VA hospital told the clerk that he was an ex-POW. She responded, "Oh, you are one of those who refused to fight." Other former prisoners of war report remarks made by neighbors or associates implying that being captured in battle was something less than honorable. In a recent exchange of letters in a national veterans magazine, one man wrote that he would place little reliance on anything said by someone who had been captured twice by the enemy.

These insulting and belittling remarks are heard with enough frequency to suggest fairly widespread misunderstanding of the prisoner of war experience. Many people seem to believe that it could not happen to them. In their view, apparently, a brave and conscientious man would never surrender.

Not only are such beliefs wrong, they are also demeaning to the many brave men who fought with distinction before they were taken captive by enemy forces. More to the point, it is dangerous for our fighting men to harbor such distorted views about a subject which could be of vital importance to them. Current and future members of our armed forces should have a clear understanding of the circumstances which could lead to their capture in wartime. They should know also what the consequences of surrender are likely to be for them. It would be a terrible mistake for them to go into battle believing that surrender is an outcome they never need contemplate. It would be an even greater mistake for them to think surrender would bring to an end the terror, rage, and fatigue they associate with combat.

Understanding the Ex-POW Psyche

Hearing their Silence

It is easy to see why the public is not better-informed about the prisoner of war experience. Those who are best able to supply that information are the ones who are least likely to talk about it. The former prisoner of war does not often reveal that status to others. Some ex-POWs have never told their own families that they were once prisoners of war. There are good reasons for their reticence.

The attempts to talk about prison camp experiences have been, for many of us, too painful. The words rekindle the horrors we have tried to forget. When we try to recount those events to others, we find ourselves weeping and incoherent, unable to continue. Some have tried to answer honestly the queries of concerned relatives, only to be disbelieved. People with no combat experience could not fathom that supposedly civilized men could behave in the ways we have witnessed. After I described to a neighbor how the Japanese mistreated me, he said, "I would never have stood for that!"

Most of the ex-POWs I know, husbands and fathers, do not want to expose their loved ones, even vicariously, to the suffering they endured in prison camps. They have also learned that words alone cannot convey the true nature of those experiences. People who have never missed more than a few meals in their lifetimes do not understand what years of starvation can do to men's minds and bodies. As a consequence, ex-POWs tend to avoid those occasions when they might be called upon to speak about those bleak years.

The POW Experience

If they were asked to address uniformed personnel about the questions of surrender and captivity, there are some things former prisoners of war could say – profound truths that would generate little disagreement among those who have shared those circumstances. They would say that surrender is not always a way to escape the hazards of the battlefield. Conditions are such on the field of combat that it is not always feasible to take prisoners or to care for them after their capture. Many who surrender in combat are killed as soon as they put down their weapons. Frequently, other prisoners are executed en route to places of detention. Before a prisoner ever reaches a prison camp, he can be expected to be physically abused, deprived of necessary food and water, exposed to inclement weather, and marched to exhaustion.

The infamous Bataan Death March, a truly barbaric event, was not an isolated example of this kind of mistreatment. In Germany, for lack of transport, groups of Allied prisoners were marched long distances and for long periods of time to evade recapture by advancing friendly forces. In Korea, many captured U.N. troops were force-marched in bitterly cold weather without food, shelter, or medical treatment to camps far removed from the battle zone. Many of the prisoners, sometimes the majority of them, did not survive these grueling ordeals.

Nor can those who surrender in battle depend upon their captors to protect them from outside attack. Not only do enraged mobs of civilians occasionally attack the escorted prisoners, they are also shelled, bombed, strafed, and torpedoed by friendly forces while on the march or while being transported in unmarked trucks, trains or ships. It should be noted that American servicemen wounded in such attacks are not eligible for the Purple Heart award because their injuries were not inflicted by the enemy.[2]

Captured personnel are no safer behind prison walls. Some people have the idea that prison camps are places of relative safety, where boredom is the major complaint. They could gain such an impression from the fictionalized accounts of prison camps portrayed in movies and on television. Maybe they have heard about the Geneva Convention and they assume that prisoners of war are treated according to its humane provisions. In World War II, when Bataan surrendered, more

"When I write, I sense that the ghosts of dead men are peering over my shoulder, nodding approvingly or, communicating to my brain in some unearthly way, that what I've just written is not quite the way it was. It's an eerie feeling, I'll clue you. At times, the feeling of another presence is so intense that I must stop and leave the house. And my body plods on mechanically, while it waits for reason to return, and then I'm afraid that madness is very near."
Robert V. Larson
Plymouth, Minnesota

3

than 10,000 men were taken prisoner by the Japanese. At the end of that war, only about one-third of that number were still alive.[3] They did not die of boredom.

In some of the German camps and routinely in the camps operated by the Japanese, enlisted personnel were used as slave labor. Dirty, dangerous work was assigned to them. They were overworked, starved, tortured, denied medical treatment, beaten, inadequately clothed, housed in unheated buildings, prevented from communicating with their families, kept in ignorance about the progress of the war, and placed in unmarked buildings adjacent to military installations that were subject to attacks by Allied aircraft.

Some people may believe that a prison camp is a safer place than a battlefield and much more comfortable. Many of us who have been in both places would choose the battlefield, without hesitation, over some of the places where we have been held in captivity.

Those prisoners who do survive the war cannot be assured of a return to friendly hands. Even today, large numbers of servicemen are listed as missing in action, although there is reason to believe that many of them were taken prisoner. Some of the Allied troops liberated from prison camps in Eastern Europe and many of the airmen who parachuted from crippled aircraft were imprisoned by the Russians when they fell into their hands during World War II. It is believed that thousands of these men just disappeared. And live sightings of American personnel still are reported from the areas under attack during the Vietnam conflict. Clearly, surrendering as a prisoner of war is an undertaking fraught with danger at every stage.

After the War: Long-Term Effects

"The first rice we received, about 3/4 cup, had a few small worms boiled in it, and many of us promptly discarded the entire bowl. However, the Wake Island Marines and civilians took what we discarded and ate it with relish. Before long, we took our ration of rice and picked out the worms and ate the rest. Finally we just ate it all, thankful that we might be getting a little protein too. One day we found a rat (head, skin, guts and all) boiled in the rice and the men actually raffled it off. I didn't win."

John W. Whipple
Tacoma, Washington

Liberation does not mean that the prisoner of war is really free. A very large proportion, if not all, of those who survived the more brutal camps of Germany, Japan, Korea, and Vietnam have not recovered from the effects of that experience. In addition to physical ailments, many have a chronic form of post traumatic stress disorder.[4] These are not the kind of injuries which are easily recognized or widely understood.

Former prisoners of war tend to be nervous, withdrawn, hostile, restless, and paranoid. Sexual dysfunctions are a common complaint, along with nightmares, flashbacks, and an inability to concentrate. These men have difficulty in establishing strong emotional ties with others, they sleep poorly, they are irritable, and they may have trouble controlling their tempers. Depression and a tendency to cry at inappropriate times are other characteristics of ex-POWs.[5]

Generally these men tend to avoid associating with people and events

4

which might awaken memories of their dark pasts. Many of them are socially isolated, lonely individuals with few friends, often estranged from their families. Accidents and suicide claimed a large proportion of these survivors in the years immediately after their release, and many others have succumbed to alcoholism and disease.[6] Of those alive today, few ex-POWs could claim to be living without aftereffects from their imprisonment experiences.

When Fighting Men Surrender

With that background in mind, it might be useful now to look at the circumstances which led to the surrender of many of the men who were captured in World War II. The groups cited here are fairly representative of the American servicemen who were taken prisoner in that war. It is interesting to conjecture to what extent these real fighting men correspond to the popular notion that only quitters allow themselves to be captured. How many of these men who laid down their arms could have escaped capture?

Wake Island
The circumstances which led to my own capture in World War II were not unusual. I was a young Marine helping to fortify Wake Island when war came upon us before we were prepared. Following the sudden strike against Pearl Harbor, we withstood 16 days of bombing attacks and we beat off one invasion attempt by a naval task force. However, the Japanese returned with enough firepower and manpower to overcome any resistance we might be able to mount. In the ensuing battle, with enemy warships encircling our tiny island, it became obvious that we could not hold out against such superior forces.

While our small Marine detachment of less than 500 men was prepared to go down fighting, there were about 1,200 unarmed civilian construction workers to be considered. They would be annihilated if the Marines held on to the bitter end. To prevent such a slaughter, our commanding officer ordered us to surrender. Marines wept and cursed when they heard that order. We had not been defeated and none of us thought it possible that Marines would surrender under any conditions. But because we were trained to obey orders, we surrendered. I am prepared to take issue with anyone who suggests that we quit for lack of will or courage.[7]

Guam
On Guam, another Pacific outpost, no provision was made to equip that island to withstand a determined assault. The token Marine garrison had neither the manpower nor the weapons to defend the island against a planned invasion. The island and its small Marine detachment were captured, but not because its defenders were lacking

in fighting spirit. They became prisoners of war because of decisions made earlier in Washington that these small islands would not be armed to repel a full-scale invasion effort.[8]

China

Another small group of our fighting men were captured in China at the beginning of WWII because of decisions made by others far from the scene. The North China Marines were legation guards and were considered a part of the embassy staff. They were armed only with rifles and pistols and they lived in a city which was under the military control of the Japanese. At first, they were interned, pending repatriation, along with other diplomatic personnel. When it became evident that the State Department would do nothing to ensure their recognition as members of the diplomatic staff, the Japanese made them ordinary prisoners of war. It is hard to see what they could have done to escape incarceration after they were abandoned by their leaders in Washington.[9]

Philippines

The largest number of American fighting men were captured in World War II when the Japanese invaded the Philippines and conquered Bataan and Corregidor. Our men fought long and valiantly, receiving neither reinforcements nor supplies. After months of combat, they ran out of food, ammunition, equipment, weapons, and medical supplies. When their commanding officers made the decision to surrender, the men were hungry (having been reduced to two small meals a day) and exhausted; large numbers of them suffered from malnutrition, dysentery, malaria, dengue, beriberi, and scurvy.

The decision to surrender the American forces in the Philippines was inescapable. Military strategists in Washington gave first priority to the war in Europe and the defeat of Germany; military resources in the Pacific were too limited to risk them in rescuing the Philippines. Surrender was not the result of disheartened and frightened troops giving up on a battle they should have continued: those men were sacrificed deliberately when distant leaders decided that they were expendable.[10]

Battle of the Bulge

Another large batch of prisoners was taken in the Battle of the Bulge. The retreating Germans caught the Allied forces by surprise when they mounted a tank-led counterattack in such strength that they broke through and penetrated deeply behind our defensive lines. It was a time of mass confusion, bitter cold weather, poor visibility, disrupted communications, and disintegrating command structures. Seasoned fighting men were cut off from their units and found themselves isolated and surrounded by enemy armor. Large units were surrendered by their officers, while others, without adequate means to defend their positions, were swept up by the rapidly advancing German army. It is not likely that many of these men made individual decisions to surrender because they lacked the will to resist.[11]

"My husband was a prisoner of the Germans and was held in Stalag Luft-1 on the Baltic Sea in Barth, Germany for 18 months. I was 23 years old when we married in 1952 and my life has been a living hell since. I had never heard of post traumatic stress disorder and therefore spent a lifetime trying to find out what went wrong in our marriage. We moved from place to place, job to job, and nothing ever made him happy. He could never work for anyone else. He would go on alcoholic binges, and was very abusive verbally and physically. In 1958 he tried to commit suicide."

*Anne L. Massey
Greenville, Mississippi*

American Airmen

Prisoner of war ranks were swelled further by the large number of American airmen who were shot down by enemy fire. Many of these men parachuted into enemy territory and were captured as soon as they landed. Some were so badly wounded that they could take no evasive action. Men fleeing from burning and exploding aircraft over blazing target areas had little chance to avoid imprisonment, if they reached the ground safely.[12]

The seemingly popular notion that American fighting men do not surrender, unless they are quitters, is not borne out by the evidence reviewed here. It seems that the majority of those who were taken prisoner had little or no choice in the matter. Prisoners of war fall generally into two categories. There are those who are wounded or otherwise unable to escape capture when their positions are overrun or they are forced to bail out of damaged aircraft. Then there are those who are positioned by their leaders in places of maximum danger without the equipment, supplies, and manpower needed to hold those positions under assault by the enemy. Most of those in the latter group, which was the largest group in World War II, are lost by design, since it is known in advance that they would be killed or captured in the event of full-scale war.

The Survivors

When you see a former prisoner of war, you are seeing a combat veteran. Because of a decision made for him by others, in most cases, he was sentenced to an indeterminate term in a foreign prison with no time off for good behavior and no visiting hours.

With few exceptions, the prisoner of war was treated cruelly by his captors. Large numbers of his buddies died in prison camps of malnutrition, disease, starvation, execution, untreated injuries, casual brutality, bombings, or work-related accidents. He is a survivor haunted by memories of experiences which, even now, affect his daily relations with his family and friends, his earning power, and his longevity. Most of these ex-POWs can report that they have received no recognition or special reward for the punishment they survived in the defense of their country. Relatively few of these men have even been compensated for the disabling injuries they sustained as prisoners of war.[13]

Former prisoners of war can tell you that surrender is a passport to hell. From their bitter experience we can learn that there are indeed worse fates than death. Surrender, they will tell you, is what you do only when all other options are closed. Even then, surrender may not be the least painful solution to a no-win situation. Even if you should survive the imprisonment experience, they can attest that you will never again be free.

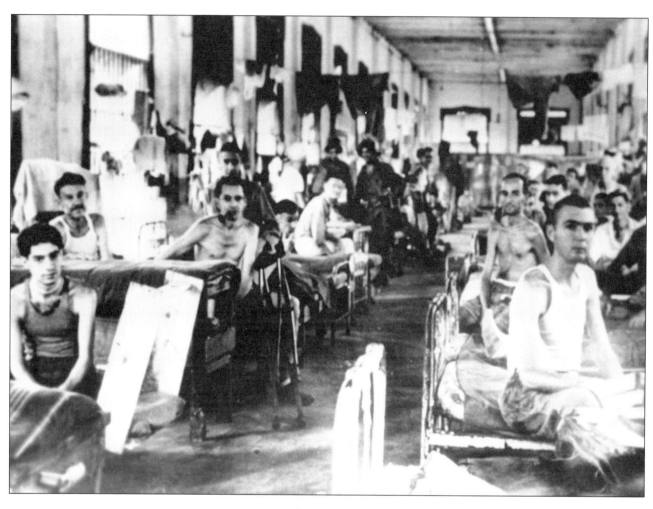

Bilibid POW hospital ward, Philippine Islands. Courtesy of American Ex-Prisoners of War, Inc.

Anger and the Ex-POW

In the Japanese prison camps, where I was held captive, the threat of death was a daily prospect, whether by accident, execution, casual brutality, starvation, or illness. We were starved and overworked, slated for certain death by pre-invasion execution or starvation in the coal mines of Hokkaido. Only the atomic bomb saved us from that fate.[1]

But we were saved, and we did survive. Those of us who lived through those years went on to lead apparently normal lives, with only a few behavioral or health differences to separate us from the general population.

Why, then, do I and other ex-POWs still suffer emotionally from prison camp experiences more than 40 years in our past? Why do we still wake up screaming, why do we have difficulty in our relationships, why do we have so much trouble expressing simple human emotion?

I have no expertise as a psychologist and I make no pretensions of learning in mental health theory. Nevertheless, I believe that my efforts to understand my prison camp legacy may help others who are similarly afflicted to gain insight into their own difficulties.

Diagnosis and Adjustment

We came home as part of a large mob of demobilized troops, with little notice and with no special attention to our adjustment problems. In my own case, I recall that nightmares, nervous tremors, paranoia, depression, and crying episodes caused me to seek medical advice when I returned to the Great Lakes Naval Hospital after my repatriation leave. Hospitalized for observation because of my complaints, I was later discharged honorably from the Marine Corps as unfit for further military duty. Because the American Red Cross took an interest in my case, I was awarded a disability rating of 50% at the time of my discharge. My disability was diagnosed as anxiety neurosis. Today, the diagnosis would have been post traumatic stress disorder (PTSD).

Anxiety neurosis/PTSD is a common affliction of former prisoners of war.[2] Many of us with that diagnosis do not understand the illness. We are not able to say just what is wrong with us and we do not

"I feel like a rape victim, although I have never been subjected to forced sexual intercourse or sodomy. I have, however, been subjected to all the other conditions of rape victims; I have suffered the physical brutality of a stronger force, I have been forced to do things and act in ways I did not want to act, I have been defiled, spat upon, and degraded, as have rape victims, except that my ordeal did not last 30 minutes or an hour, but almost 33,000 hours. And like the rape victim who was told, 'You are partially to blame, you provoked him, or, you didn't fight hard enough, or you must have wanted it,' people have looked at the POW and said, 'You must have been a coward, because you surrendered instead of fighting, or you must have wanted to be a POW or you would have done something to prevent it or to end it'."

John W. Whipple
Tacoma, Washington

11

understand why we are that way. Most of us, I suspect, would tend to deny that we are especially anxious or neurotic. For several years after liberation, it is true that I had problems of adjustment, but by 1960, 15 years later, I was able to put aside my identification as an ex-POW and to see myself primarily in terms of my work role. I believed that my behavior then was normal and that I no longer had any adjustment problems.

And, like most of us, I told myself that I had no grudge against the Japanese people. Whenever questioned about it, I would absolve the Japanese people for the crimes committed by their military leaders. I believed that one should forget the cruelties of the past, that it was un-Christian and neurotic to harbor thoughts of revenge for ancient wrongs. In my efforts to come to a peaceful resolution of my past, I acted sincerely. I believed I was doing what was both right and necessary. So far as I could tell, I had no problem in coming to terms with my prison camp experiences.

Shouldn't I Be Angry?

It wasn't until 1974 that I began to suspect I might have a more serious problem than I realized in shedding my prison camp history. I found myself abroad at a business lunch which included a Japanese gentleman of my age who spoke excellent English. He was a pleasant and gracious lunch partner and I enjoyed his manner and his stories. We found that we had mutual acquaintances at a university in the United States where he had taken postgraduate work. Before long, I noticed that I was getting nervous for no reason that I could determine. My hands started to tremble and then my whole body began to shake. In embarrassment, I excused myself and left the room.

Later it occurred to me that, in the back of my mind, I may have been speculating about the wartime activities of that man who was my age. When I related that incident to my wife and tried to tell her how I felt about the way the Japanese had treated us in captivity, I broke down and wept, unable to continue.

Naturally, I was shaken by my behavior and I could not explain it. The events I spoke about had taken place 30 years ago. How could I be so emotional about something that had happened so long ago? Why was I unable to tell my wife, a sympathetic listener, anything about that period of my life? So far as I can recall, I had done nothing in prison camp that I would be ashamed to recall or that I would fear to confess. Knowing that I had no animosity toward the Japanese, why did that Japanese gentleman make me so nervous?

My first insight came to me when I was reading a novel by James Jones, who wrote a number of fiction stories based on his experiences as a

"I want to thank Dr. Kelnhofer for (his) article. I too have hidden anger and have kept my depression hidden for many, many years. I too still have nightmares. In my awakening mind I see the buddies being buried alive. How we were laughed at by the Germans when we had to have a bowel movement in the middle of the street. I was beaten, thrown on the side of the road to die because I was too weak to walk. I remember very well eating from garbage cans, paying $78 for four potatoes, swapped two for a cigarette. When I have to go to the VA Hospital I always get mad and upset at the way I am treated and talked to. On the other hand, I've been told by the VA in Montgomery that my POW (experience) was not the cause of my nerves. How sad. If only the people that make the rules had been there. I hope before the end of all POWs' life journey there will be some compensation."

Wallace Delbert Carroll
Bessemer, Alabama

combat soldier in the Pacific during World War II. In the story, a young soldier confesses to his sergeant that he is ashamed of his behavior in battle because he lost control of his anger. The older man tells him that he behaved normally and had done nothing to be ashamed of. He says that the young man must remember that he is, after all, only a human being and not an automatic fighting machine. As a human being, he advised him, it is perfectly natural to express rage and to be overcome with anger.[3]

As I read that passage, I realized that I had made the same mistake as the character in Jones' novel. I had denied myself the right to have normal human emotions about what had been done to me and to my comrades by the Japanese. It was only natural that I should be angry at the Japanese guards. It was perfectly human of me to want revenge for the injuries they had caused me. Instead of recognizing and admitting my hatred and my rage, I had denied those feelings because they conflicted with my social training. I had been taught as a child and counseled as an adult that it is wrong to hold a grudge and that it is right to forgive one's enemies. For the most part, I was successful, I thought, in forgiving the unforgivable and forgetting the unforgettable experiences of my years of captivity.

James Jones made me see that I was first of all a human being and not a forgiving angel. I was able to live with my anger and my hatred only because they had been buried so deeply in my subconscious that I was not aware of the burden I carried. I finally realized that under my veneer of a forgiving Christian gentleman, I was filled with suppressed rage and I hungered for revenge. But even while I came to understand how much anger I had bottled up inside myself, I realized I still couldn't feel it. My anger was there – it had to be – but it was out of sight and out of mind, secret and hidden from my consciousness.

Hiding Anger to Survive

One of the first lessons of survival we learned in Japanese prison camps was to show no resistance and to hide all traces of anger or disapproval. We learned to be docile and uncomplaining in the face of extreme provocation. Where the normal human reaction to a blow is to strike back, we learned not only to repress that reaction but also to repress the emotion that would prompt such a response. Where it is only natural to show anger when one is abused unjustly, we learned to accept indignities, even pain, without displaying any emotion. Eventually, after suppressing our natural feelings every day in captivity, it became an automatic response, enabling us to endure discomfort and physical punishment without thinking. We became accustomed to behaving in ways that were not normal until the abnormal became our norm for survival.

"Finally, after 45 years, I understand why my behavior is abnormal in comparison with the rest of society. This enlightenment comes thanks to the exceptional article by Guy Kelnhofer, Jr. Mr. Kelnhofer's characteristics duplicate mine without exception. His fine disclosure of his own problems has lifted a burden off my shoulders."
Ward Gardner
Palisade, Colorado

13

To an outsider, we appeared to be subhuman creatures, acting as automatons in circumstances where ordinary men would have been rebellious and hostile. Aviators who were shot down later in the war confided that their first impression on entering our camp was that we were all deranged. If we failed to react as ordinary men would to the abuses we suffered, does that mean that we did not feel the blows and that we did not resent our unearned punishments? Did we come to accept the cruelties of our guards as right and proper? My own recollection is that we were just as enraged at injustice and abuse after three years as we were after one week of captivity. We were no longer surprised by it, nor were we as unprepared to survive such a regime as at the beginning, but we still felt the hurts and resented them as deeply as before. We never considered the starvation, overwork, and beatings as normal and acceptable behavior. I do not remember being so inured to brutality that I did not entertain myself with fantasies of revenge from time to time.

So what happened to all those secret vows of retribution each of us swore as he witnessed or suffered some brutal indignity? What happened to all those surges of anger that we were forced to repress so often for so many years? Can anyone bottle up so much anger, hidden as it may be, without having it affect his life and his behavior? No. We are feeling, normal human beings, no more able to seal ourselves off from pain and suffering than other people. We bleed, we hurt, and we cry like anyone else. But we are different, in that we have learned to conceal from others, and, finally, from ourselves, our reaction to the suffering we have known.

A Life Without Emotion

So how did the deeply repressed anger affect the way we lived after our liberation? I cannot tell how it affected others but, in time, I came to see how it influenced my life. For me, one consequence of repressing my feelings was that I became emotionally numb, rendering unresponsive some inner core of my being. I could witness joy and spontaneous happiness in others, but I could not emulate it in my own life. My ability to feel strong emotions had dulled, and my life became more serious because of it.

Without noticing it, I became internally sensitive to interpersonal conflicts and antagonisms. I began to take steps to avoid the prospects of confrontation with real or potential antagonists, never realizing I was doing it. Looking back, my work record reveals a pattern of conflict avoidance, with new jobs every two or three years. I always thought I had good, compelling reasons for my moves, but after 30 years of changes, I know now that I was running away from something. The fear that drove me, I believe, was the fear that I might lose

"Most of the things that made me a poor employee can be traced directly back to my POW experiences. I am angry, I get easily frustrated, I am intolerant of inefficiency and complacency among bureaucratic clerks, I resent employees who use sick leave for the slightest reason, I seek perfection, I don't make or have close friends, I am emotionally flat. I have finally used up all of my reserves – I can't start the things I know must be done, I can't finish what I start. I have been blamed for each of those things most of my life since I was a POW. In fact, I grew to believe that those character faults were my own responsibility, and that if I could just think positively, I would overcome all of those bad things. I was told that I was almost unique – only a few undesirable citizens were as angry as I. It wasn't until I got in a POW therapy group at the VAMC, Seattle, that I learned that almost all the other POWs have the same anger and most of the other symptoms."

John W. Whipple
Tacoma, Washington

14

control of my anger. Both the fear and the anger, however, are de-
duced. Neither are felt by me at the conscious level where I might
subdue them with logic and reasoned argument.

What this tells me is that all of us, normal human beings, not angels
or demigods, were deeply offended and terribly angered by what the
Japanese did to us and to our helpless comrades. We hid that anger and
controlled it so well that we banished it from our consciousness. Now
we should know why we trembled and shook, why our muscles knot-
ted, why we screamed in the night. Inside each of us is a caged tiger
of hate, anger, and outrage. That tiger thirsts for revenge, for the blood
of those who made us suffer so cruelly and for so many years. That
ravening beast is securely locked up and there is little chance that he
will ever escape to do his bloody work. But every now and then, when
someone does us an injury or threatens our welfare, the beast stirs and
he begins to claw at his restraints, smelling the enemy again.

If this hidden reservoir of anger is a handicap, then it is one of many
which are the natural legacy of our prison camp experiences. Holding
in anger can be a reason for shaky hands and tremulous voices;[4] depression has often been called anger turned inward.[5] Knowing what it
is that makes us touchy, irritable, restless, and depressed may make
it easier to control. Perhaps it will also make us less likely to place the
blame outside of ourselves, on our wives, our children, and our
neighbors.

Former prisoners of war are not the only ones to experience this anger.
Victims of Nazi concentration camps, battered wives, abused children,
and subjects of racial and religious persecution all have similar reason
to conceal and, in time, forget, the heavy burden of hate and anger
accumulated from years of brutal treatment. Their anger, like ours,
comes from years of unresisting acceptance of physically and mentally
abusive behavior by individuals or groups who had life or death
power over them.

I write this to open the minds of those who deal with former prisoners
of war in a therapeutic relationship. It has been my experience that
very few mental health professionals realize that we are angry and that
we have just cause for the anger we carry. To be effective, our counselors must put aside the simplistic notion that we can accept their
advice to forgive our enemies and find peace by renouncing our anger.
Would that it were so easy.

There is no way to rid ourselves of that caged tiger because he is too
well concealed for us to find him and give him a peaceful end. We will
always carry that secret passenger in the deep, dark recesses of our
spirits, waiting for the revenge forever denied to us.

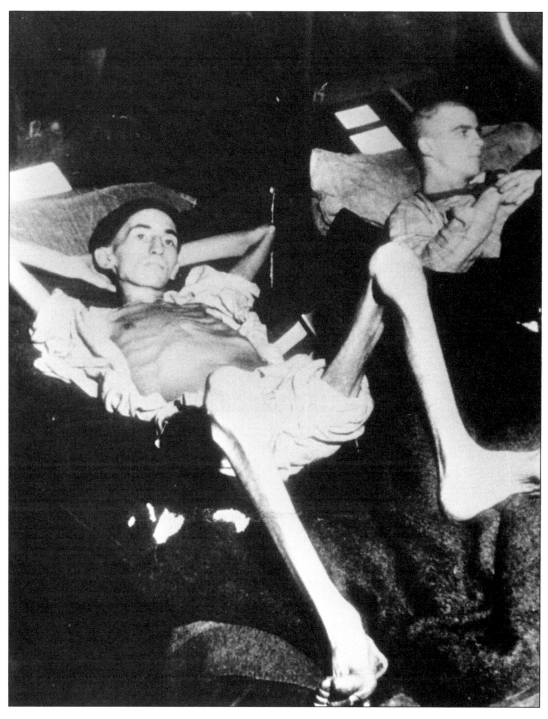

A GI is liberated from German prison camp.   Courtesy of American Ex-Prisoners of War, Inc.

You Don't Look Disabled To Me

What does it mean to have that cluster of symptoms which are common to the survivors of death camps? In what way are the survivors in this illness category handicapped by those experiences? For the most part, their injuries are not visible. This is partly a consequence of the dissembling behavior which is practiced without conscious intent by these former inmates: they appear to be neat, pleasant and unassuming, even quiet and reserved in their demeanor. Inwardly, however, their prison conditioning ensures that they will maintain a rigid control of their emotions.

Their families are likely to find these survivors to be irritable, frequently angry, restless, uncommunicative, withdrawn, secretive, wary, depressed, and unsociable. Survivors with those characteristics who manage to achieve some measure of success, therefore, are likely to do so only at the price of pretending and role-playing. This emotional masquerade requires a constant vigilance and a steady expenditure of nervous energy which tends to feed their depression. Reliance on alcohol and other drugs often follows naturally as the survivors strive to maintain a public persona which is not supported by their emotions.[1]

None of these disabling effects is easily discernible, even to the survivors themselves. The results, however, are at least as crippling as any physical injury could ever be. If former prisoners of war are to be properly diagnosed and treated, it is essential to first understand their symptoms and the reasons for their behavior. Following is a discussion of those symptoms, and of the costs already exacted by injuries, visible and otherwise.

Disabled? Really?

As a consequence of injuries received while a prisoner of the Japanese, from 1941 to 1945, I am rated 100% disabled by the Department of Veterans Affairs. As a matter of fact, my multiple disabilities added up to 220% in the evaluations made by the DVA physicians. However, I have lost none of my limbs. Neither am I blind or badly disfigured. My disabilities are not visible ones.

A physician who was once a guest at my dinner table was surprised to learn that I am totally disabled, as he could see no outward sign of

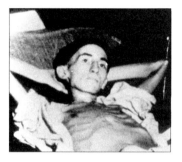

"We have been married 42 years and out of these there are but a very few months when there was less stress. For 38 years I have been his nurse, manager in all respects. He needs constant direction. As you say, friends, neighbors, and even clergy do not completely understand. They do not share the constant confusion, frustrations, and the sadness which is always there. To think that I must order this most accomplished man to: Wash your hair! Come now, you must have your shower . . . then see to it that he dresses without his pajamas under his trousers. When he is seen by neighbors, friends and clergy, impeccably dressed, no one knows what our private life is like."

Geraldine Meek
Sun City, Arizona

my handicaps. Had he been a little more observant, he would have noticed the hearing aid in my left ear, although he would not have known from that how little hearing remains in my other ear. It amazes me that most of the young medical residents with whom I come in contact will think of childhood illnesses and other possible causes of hearing impairment, but will ignore the effects of starvation on the auditory nerves. Not many doctors today would be ready to believe that the Japanese would deliberately injure and starve American prisoners of war.

Fortunately, one of my other illnesses was in transient remission, or I would not have risked being there at all. This affliction causes me to lose my equilibrium completely for just a few seconds. During that short interval, I fall to the floor, even when I am seated in a chair. These attacks occur without any warning, at any time and in any place; there seems to be no pattern or any initiating cause so I am always vulnerable. No medication has been found that can prevent the attacks or mitigate their effects. Although this is a serious disability, it is not usually a visible one.

Another disability, which I share with most ex-POWs, is called "anxiety neurosis," a psychiatric label used in the 1940s to explain the symptoms exhibited by combat veterans and by returning prisoners of war. This category of mental illness was replaced during the Vietnam War by post traumatic stress disorder, or PTSD. In Europe, where psychiatrists had to deal with large numbers of survivors of the concentration camps, they designed a new category of mental illness, called the "KZ Syndrome".[2] During World War II, a relatively large number of prisoners of war, particularly those taken captive by Asian forces, were imprisoned under conditions roughly similar to those found in the concentration camps of Europe in World War II. As can be expected, therefore, the prisoners of war who survived those imprisonment conditions also suffered from a pervasive traumatic experience, similar – if not identical to – KZ Syndrome. Since the American psychiatrists do not have such a category of mental illness in their professional manuals, some American survivors of World War II still carry the diagnosis of anxiety neurosis while the ex-POWs of the Vietnam War are diagnosed with post traumatic stress disorder.

(In)visible Symptoms Common to Survivors

Psychic Numbing
Perhaps the most common and least recognized handicap faced by survivors is a condition known as "psychic numbing". Since survival in the camps could be seriously threatened by outward displays of emotion such as anger or fear, it became vital to suppress such normal reactions. The survivors learned to stifle those reactions by eliminating the feelings that caused them. Over the years of incarceration, this

suppression of one's true emotions became a form of extreme conditioning, one which shaped the behavior of the prisoners without any thought or conscious direction from them. It remains an unconscious personality trait of the survivors of these camps. Since it is not a consciously adopted coping mechanism, it cannot be discarded when it no longer serves a useful purpose. The effect of psychic numbing is described by some survivors as a kind of inner death, and they see themselves as hollow men. There are no outward signs of this disability.

There may be no recognizable monetary cost to psychic numbing, but it does represent a very high personal loss. To be filled with joy, to be excitedly happy on graduation, on being married, on achieving a promotion, on the birth of a child, or on celebrating an anniversary – these are not common responses for those afflicted with psychic numbing. One is more likely to find them standing dry-eyed at the burial of a loved one or reacting with calm equanimity when accidents or serious illnesses threaten the lives of family members; such are the responses learned from years of brutal punishment as prisoners of war or as inmates of concentration camps.[3]

Depression

Another disability not evident to the untrained eye is a chronic, but sub-acute form of depression. It is marked by apathy and a loss of interest in persons who once commanded our attention and in activities which once consumed a large part of our nonworking hours. Chronically depressed people tend to lead drab, uninteresting lives, devoid of concern or involvement with causes or current events. Many have weathered attacks of acute depression in which they descend into a bottomless pit of despair with no hope, ambition, or interest to arrest the descent. Repeated attacks of this severity can lead to suicide.[4]

Fatigue

Excessive fatigue is commonly found in the survivors of these death camps. In the grip of this symptom, they might sleep for days without interruption, or from 3 p.m. until 7 a.m. day after day for a period of weeks. They might find their arms too heavy to lift, or request to be taken home from work, too fatigued to drive even a short distance. These periods of excessive fatigue may be infrequent or of short duration. The illness is extremely disabling but, again, it is not a visible disability.[5]

Neuropathy

One of the more widely-recognized effects of prolonged periods of vitamin deficiency is peripheral neuropathy. In this condition, there is a burning and painful sensation in the lower extremities.[6] For me, one of the manifestations is extreme foot pain when walking. I have found that this pain can be avoided if I dose myself daily with pantothetic acid, a non-prescription vitamin. Without that medication, how-

"From Ashland, California (after liberation), I was transferred to the U.S. Naval Air Station Hospital in Memphis, Tennessee, and while I was at home on a short leave I broke down and cried, because my mother and father raised their voices at each other. I also broke down and cried before the Naval officer in charge of my work, but I do not believe any of this was put in my medical file."
Otis T. Jones
Gainesville, Florida

21

ever, my disability would be readily apparent from my painful and tentative way of walking.

Myoclonus

Spouses are aware of those forms of disability that appear when the survivors are sleeping. They notice that their ex-POW spouses tend to jerk and twitch spasmodically when they are at rest. This condition is known as myoclonus. Nightmares, in which they relive old horrors or imagine new terrors of pursuit, capture, and torture, still haunt their sleep even decades after liberation. The sleep of the survivors is interrupted frequently, for no apparent reason. Perhaps it is an unconscious need to check out their environment lest dangers creep up on them in the dark.[7]

Sexual Dysfunction

Sexual dysfunction in the form of impotence is a common complaint of the ex-POW. Although there are no statistics on its prevalence in this population, conversations with hundreds of these survivors gives the impression that it is a disability affecting the majority of them. This is another factor having negative consequences on the marriages of the survivors. While this disability would be difficult to measure in economic terms, it detracts significantly from their social welfare.

The Measurable Costs

Financial Loss

For those survivors who had accumulated educational benefits under the GI Bill, one monetary cost of their experience is easy to assess. In essence, many lost their GI Bill benefits because their symptoms would not permit them to study or concentrate. After liberation, former prisoners found their memory capacities were reduced, and they were too restless to sit quietly in classrooms or too hostile to submit to academic discipline. Further, many were disoriented from dependence on alcohol or exhausted from sleep disturbances caused by nightmares and flashbacks of imprisonment experiences.

Other survivors have been economically penalized because of excessive mobility, moving from job to job or city to city every few years. Some could not rise in their chosen fields because they could not get along with co-workers or supervisors. Many retired early when they found the stresses of their work becoming unbearable and their employers ever more dissatisfied. There are no outward signs marking these people as handicapped in the economic race.

There are other costs for these survivors. Retirement left many without the refuge of a workplace to escape the emotional demands of families.

"There is no simple answer to what impact prison had on us. In the air crews we were, on the whole, the most healthy, bright, and stable the military had at its disposal. I understand that there were 26,000 Army Air Corps POWs. None of us even wore glasses; our teeth even had to be nearly perfect. Yet, we are dying off sooner than the general population and have more problems."
Charles Williams
Greenbank, Washington

One characteristic shared by these prison camp survivors is their excessive devotion to their work. Many of them became workaholics. This pattern of emotional and physical withdrawal from families and spouses had its negative effects on their marriages and on the mental health of their children.

Loss of Government Compensation

Large numbers of these disabled veterans have found it impossible to obtain compensation from the government for their service-connected injuries. This is due in part to their inability to handle the emotional stress associated with the required tests. Few of them have had the stamina to pursue their claims through all of the administrative channels provided in the compensation system. For many of these former prisoners of war, denial and suppression have been their primary coping mechanisms, prompting them to avoid people or events that stimulate memories of the suffering they endure. Some find that they are unable to complete the personal histories required for compensation claims. Even those who take an active part in veterans activities may not have the emotional strength needed to press the claim for proper compensation.[8]

Costs to the Family

Living with a former prisoner of war can have a profound effect on families. Job loss, due to frequent illness or to alcoholism, may require another family member to take up part-time employment to maintain the household income. If the survivor won't make use of free medical care for veterans, the family may struggle with unnecessary medical bills. The wife may be called upon to provide in-home nursing services for her husband. In the face of these responsibilities, she is not able to earn the seniority and the experience necessary in her job for promotion and pension benefits. Her role as nurse and provider also prevents her from enrolling in and completing educational courses which could prepare her for more remunerative employment. When her disabled husband dies at a relatively early age because of his poor health, she is often left with a family to support, medical and burial bills to pay, and few of the marketable skills that are needed to maintain her standard of living. Because her husband isolated himself from former prison camp comrades and other veterans, she is not likely to have the knowledge or the guidance which would allow her to make use of the benefits to which she is entitled by her status as the widow of a disabled veteran.

The Survivors Today

The survivors have lived through an intense experience during which all the foundations of their lives were destroyed. They were forced to adapt to a foreign environment – one characterized by brutality, thievery, extreme hunger, excessive thirst, exposure to the elements, vicious guards, capricious and unrestricted authority, sudden death, hard labor, cruelty, humiliations, beatings, isolation, suspicion, hatred, and uncertainty. After several years of such conditioning, the survivors returned to their homes with a mindset which reflected that formative background of training and experience. Postponement of satisfaction, for example, can be difficult for people who have been geared to live for the moment and who have had no firm expectations of a tomorrow. Prisoners who have grown accustomed to the loss of personal possessions by confiscation, destruction, and theft tend to place little value on goods and other outward signs of wealth or security. They tend to choose a corner seat with their backs to a wall because the world remains a dangerous and threatening place for them. They always keep their food larders stocked to ensure adequate supplies in an emergency.

It is natural for these survivors to feel uneasy in a crowd of strangers. It may be that they feel uncomfortably vulnerable when mingling intimately with individuals or groups whose behavior and motivation are unknown to them. Knowing how easily men can be persuaded to sacrifice others for even momentary gratifications of their hungers, they are always alert to the possibility of informants. They have learned to guard what they say and to be careful about confiding personal information to strangers. Because they have lost so many comrades and friends to murder, execution, illness, exposure, accident, and betrayal, they find it difficult to form close and intimate attachments to others. The survivors tend to be loners and to have no close friends outside of the community of ex-POWs.

The majority of ex-POWs will never have the opportunity to explain their disabilities in the way I have described them. Many of my ex-POW comrades are more gravely disabled than I am. Unlike me, they have not been properly diagnosed or compensated by the system that has been designed to care for them. If this message reaches the administrators of these medical services, perhaps it will help them to see these survivors as they truly are instead of the way they appear to be to those who are not informed about the health problems of former prisoners of war.

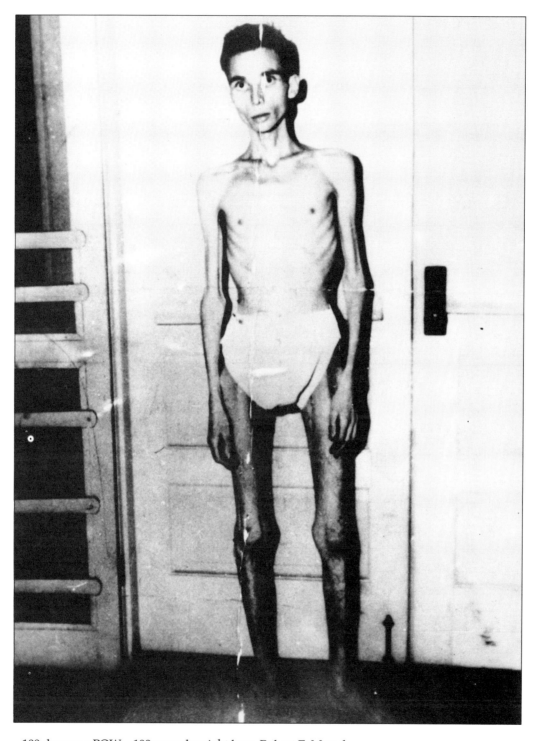

100 days as a POW – 100 pound weight loss: Robert E. Martel.   Courtesy of American Ex-Prisoners of War, Inc.

Disability Rating Problems for Ex-POWs

If one examines the disability ratings awarded by the Department of Veterans Affairs (DVA) to the prison camp survivors, it will be noted that relatively few of these men have received high ratings or adequate compensation.[1] This finding would seem to be at odds with our current medical understanding of the lifetime consequences of surviving prolonged periods of multiple physical and psychological traumas. The DVA rating pattern would lead us to believe that most of these veterans escaped the disabilities which would be expected for those who survive such traumatic circumstances. And yet we know that is not the case. It seems appropriate, therefore, to ask why more of the ex-POWs have not received ratings reflecting the damage we know must have been done to them.

The purpose of this essay is to help the DVA to develop a better understanding of the disabilities common to a large number of the former prisoners of war. It is designed also to provide guidance to those dedicated staff members in the DVA Medical Centers (VAMC) who are trying to render more effective aid to this difficult group of veterans. And perhaps the research community will find in this paper a stimulus to begin studies delineating the typical mental health consequences which follow from surviving the ordeal of living as a prisoner of war.

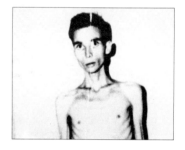

What is proposed here is not an easy task and the DVA has much pressing business to occupy its time. Still, these forgotten heroes deserve better than what they have been given so far by the DVA. Surely they have earned this little extra consideration before they pass into history. The benefits of such an undertaking will extend beyond a small number of survivors. While no one likes to consider that possibility, the future may well be filled with new ranks of ex-POWs. This exercise may establish a new and more effective way to meet the urgent health needs of returning prisoners of war.

Barriers to Compensation

Service Medical Records

A primary impediment to proper compensation for the ex-POW is the requirement that service-connected disabilities must be substantiated by the service medical record of the claimant. This is a nearly impos-

"Your comments concerning the hidden illnesses of former POWs, I believe, (are) absolutely correct. I believe very few ex-POWs ever function to their maximum abilities in life because of their experience in prison camp. They are held back by a number of things, and although they may have held down a job during their lifetime, they could have done much better without their problems. I also agree, as you know, that there are many illnesses, including mental illnesses, that have now come to the forefront as these men begin to retire."

Dr. William R. Shadish
Redding, California

sible condition for the ex-POW to meet: his service medical record does not cover the period of his imprisonment, and enemy camp commanders ordinarily did not keep and maintain such records.

The lack of records could have been offset by giving returning prisoners thorough medical examinations. However, at the conclusion of hostilities in World War II, this was not done for a number of reasons. The system was geared then for rapid demobilization. Only cursory medical exams were given to ex-POWs, most of whom had been resting and eating well in the interval between the end of hostilities and their return to Allied control. On casual inspection, therefore, most of the returning prisoners no longer displayed outward evidence of their recent ordeals. Only those with obvious physical and mental impairments were screened out for treatment or hospitalization.[2]

Those ex-POWs who might be inclined to report their less visible injuries soon realized that their homecomings could be delayed by hospitalization for an indefinite period of time. The ones who wanted to continue in military service knew that their retention and their promotion prospects would be negatively affected if they sought help for any kind of mental health problem. In their eagerness to be reunited with their families and friends, they were only too willing to overlook any injuries and illnesses which were not immediately disabling. Moreover, they saw no reason to question the prevalent medical opinion that they needed nothing more than rest and a good diet to return to the health they had once enjoyed. In most cases, nothing of significance was added to their medical service records.

No Causal Relationship

Later on, when the consequences of their imprisonment experiences began to manifest themselves in problems affecting their health and their behavior, they found that the DVA was not receptive to their complaints. The DVA took the position, as a matter of official policy, that there is no scientific proof of a causal relationship between those traumatic prison circumstances and the health problems now affecting the ex-POW community.[3] The DVA persists in this policy despite a growing consensus among many medical experts that there are serious long-term effects to be expected from the regimen of starvation, beatings, exhausting labor, exposure to the elements, and other life-threatening conditions which characterized many of the prison camps.

Congress has provided some relief for ex-POWs who cannot prove beyond a reasonable doubt that a direct relationship exists between their imprisonment experiences and a number of the most common health problems. It has instructed the DVA to consider a number of disabilities as "presumptive". That is, the DVA shall presume that certain specified disabilities are causally related to the prisoner of war experience.[4] Unfortunately, because of certain limitations and adverse interpretations, these presumptions have had little effect on the ratings awarded to the average ex-POW.

Interviewer Prejudice

The pattern of low ratings for the ex-POW can also be traced to a common misconception regarding the prisoner of war experience. Although they may be a minority, some part of the population believes that the ex-POW does not merit a disability compensation. Those people tend to regard the ex-POW as someone who refused to fight. It is their position that a brave and patriotic soldier would never surrender to the enemy. These critics do not understand that battlefield conditions do not always provide the soldier with options to exercise at his discretion. In addition, some people believe that the prison camp lives they see depicted on popular television shows represents the way prisoners were treated by their captors in real prison camps.

While any ex-POW may be subjected to criticism, few have had to face the kind of public rejection suffered by those who survived the prison camps of the Korean War. It was widely believed then that most of those men had been subtly brainwashed into embracing the cause of the enemy. Many reported that they were segregated on their return lest they infect others with their treasonous opinions. Though they had endured terrible suffering as casualties of war, many of these brave men were not welcomed home by their countrymen. The bitterness created by this unjust humiliation caused added psychic injury to men who had already been tested beyond the ordinary limits of human endurance. It is not surprising that very few of these survivors have ever surfaced to identify themselves as former prisoners of war.

So long as such questions persist about the integrity of the ex-POW community, it follows that a certain number of employees of the VAMCs will share these mistaken beliefs. Those who do so can be expected to act on their opinions when dealing with ex-POWs who come in for treatment. On the basis of such negative perceptions, some of the rating exams are going to be done by people who are prejudiced against the ex-POW.

Inadequate Interviewer Training

The ex-POW who comes to his VAMC to explain the background of his prison injuries may find it difficult to relate to those who are his examiners. There are not many in the VAMCs today who have a military background and even fewer who have had combat experience. If the examiner has never missed more than a few meals in his lifetime, what can he understand about the immediate and long-term effects on the ex-POW of years of semi-starvation? When the examiner assures an ex-POW that a little hard work never hurt anyone, he demonstrates his ignorance of the realities of slave labor in the prison camps. Words tend to lose their meaning when such common terms as "hunger" do not convey similar realities.

Today, nearly all of the ex-POWs are past middle age and the survivors of World War II prisons are old men. There is a problem for these men in communicating their uncommon experiences to those who are not only much younger, but who have had no exposure to the kinds of conditions which have shaped these prison camp survivors. The credibility of the ex-POW is compromised by these factors.

Convincing the ex-POW to expose his inner feelings is a difficult undertaking under the best conditions. Few at the VAMCs are trained to understand the power of the constraints governing the conduct of these survivors. Those who managed to survive the ordeals of prison did so by adapting themselves totally to life-threatening conditions. These behavior patterns may now be counterproductive, but they continue automatically to guide the behavior of the ex-POW. The survivor can no more divest himself of these ingrained responses than he can shed his own skin. To the VAMC examiner, the ex-POW may appear to be unduly hostile, suspicious, and withdrawn. However, ex-POWs learned the hard way to be secretive and to mask their true feelings from others. Unconsciously, they continue to conduct themselves as though the world around them is still a dangerous place.

Ex-POW Conditioning

Providing medical services to the ex-POW community is often a frustrating task. A large number of the surviving prisoners have made little or no use of the Department of Veterans Affairs.[5] They are so emotionally damaged by their prison experiences that they have elected to remain isolated from their former prison camp comrades. Instead, they try to cope by avoiding anything which might remind them of what they endured. Some of these survivors have not even confided to their spouses that they are former prisoners of war. Most of these ex-POWs are not reachable by the DVA or by any of the veterans organizations.

When an examination does take place, it is often with poor results. Frequently, ex-POWs report that their mental health exam was both short and superficial. To be effective with an ex-POW, such an exam takes hours of persistent and sympathetic probing – a regimen for which few examiners have been adequately prepared.

Some survivors who try to make use of the DVA facilities find their efforts stymied by their own conditioned resistance to speaking out.

It is not uncommon for ex-POWs to find that they are emotionally unable to undergo even routine questioning about the cause of their service-connected injuries. Many have found it beyond their ability to fill out questionnaires about their prison camp histories. Their memories are so painful that some cannot explain to the DVA examiners how they came to be injured in the course of their military service. Others, induced by their families to seek help from the local VAMC, have been rebuffed by inexperienced personnel who have rejected as unbelievable their accounts of their prison camp injuries. Many times an ex-POW has left his local VAMC, vowing never to return, because of an insensitive or rude remark made by one of the employees.

Even if the ex-POW honestly tries to reveal how he feels, he would not always be able to do so. He has blocked out of his memory and out of his consciousness the terrible fears, hatred and rages which continue to affect his performance at home and at work. Nor does he find it easy to marshal a list of physical complaints for the examiner to consider. In the prison world which molded him, men did not complain. They did not look to others for help or sympathy, but bore stoically whatever injuries and mishaps came their way. Because of this rigorous conditioning, the ex-POW is handicapped in conducting himself in the expected manner during an examination at his VAMC. It is contrary to his training as a survivor to confess a weakness or to ask others for help.

Even in a successful interview, inquiries by the medical examiner may not elicit useful information about the ex-POW's behavioral problems. The former prisoner would not often be aware of the oddities of much of his current lifestyle. The examiner could learn a great deal more about the survivor's physical and mental health problems by questioning his spouse and family. Not because he has confided in them, which is unlikely, but because they have observed him closely over a long period of time. Probably, they know him better than he knows himself.

Overcoming the Barriers

Naming the Illness

In the DVA lexicon of illnesses, there is no established medical category for that particular set of physical and psychological symptoms characteristic of the prison camp survivors. During the Vietnam conflict, post traumatic stress disorder was used to categorize the set of reactions common to single event traumas which are extraordinary in their nature and severity. However, we still have no medical category for the symptoms of those who endured prolonged periods of multiple physical and psychological torment.

Take, for example, the case of the *Oryoku Maru*, a Japanese prison ship which sailed from Manila in 1944 with some 1,600 prisoners aboard.

"I feel that many VA physicians treating us simply do not understand our background. I have had VA doctors tell me that they have heard of teachers teaching from wheelchairs. That's great, doctor. I'd like to watch you do that. Doctors, I feel, should be required to study the facts about ex-POWs. We don't want sympathy or patronizing. We do want respect for our own valor and appreciation for what we have given to them for their own security."
Charles Williams
Greenbank, Washington

The brutality and disease aboard ship were such that, upon docking, only 400 prisoners remained alive, all in wretched condition.[6] What happened to those who survived until liberation? The effects of that horrifying experience on their later physical and psychological health would be worth studying in order to define this new mental health disorder.

The prison circumstances of most prisoners of war were such that they feared for their lives on an almost daily basis. To function in such a threatening environment, the prisoners learned to adapt in ways which had to become automatic, using the mechanisms of repression and disassociation as survival skills.

The effects of such a prolonged repression of normal human emotions may be seen in the responses of these survivors to their liberation. After World War II, for example, it was found that about one-half of those who died within two years of their release from Japanese camps were victims of suicide, murder and accidents.[7] Many of those who managed to go on to lead fairly normal lives either remained in military service and/or married strong women who stayed with them and nurtured them through their painful years of readjustment.

Asking the Right Questions

When these men reach retirement age, they face new crises of identification and motivation. No longer are they able to escape the stresses of family life by using their work as a cover for their absence. Some of them come to their VAMC for help with that new adjustment. They want to know how to deal with the depression, insomnia, impotence, and failing health they are encountering. Unfortunately, they often find themselves regarded by the DVA as malingerers looking for a free ride at the taxpayer's expense. Even when they are diagnosed as suffering from chronic PTSD, the DVA would sometimes cite their retirement from an employment position as proof that the PTSD had caused them no economic disability. Few of the survivors know how to challenge such an argument and so accept a disability rating of zero compensation for their service-connected injuries.

If the DVA would look more deeply into the employment histories of these survivors, an economic penalty would be found. But first the interviewer must ask the right questions: Did the ex-POW use the education benefits accumulated under the GI Bill? Did he go on to train for a professional career (as very few ex-POWs did)? Had he been able in his employment to advance to a position in keeping with his seniority? Did he frequently change locations, employers, and residence? Was he working well below potential, considering his skills and experience? Did he retire before his time because of the increasing difficulty in getting along with co-workers, customers, subordinates, and supervisors? All of these questions indicate situations common to ex-POWs; all result in significant economic loss.[8]

Recognizing DVA Shortcomings

One reason examiners tend not to probe deeply into the backgrounds of the ex-POWs is that these survivors seem to be generally unaffected and apparently uninjured by their experiences. Their prison-formed masks and their facades of amiability hide the truth from themselves as well as from the casual inspection of others. Their ready professions of well-being are often sufficient to convince the hurried examiner that there is nothing to investigate. It is not surprising that the DVA seldom pierces such defenses to find the hidden injuries that so disable the average ex-POW. The DVA cannot be expected routinely to ferret out the secret sufferings of those evasive ex-POWs who are well enough to come in for treatment. Nor can it be judged wanting for not meeting the needs of the majority of the survivors who refuse to seek any treatment for their service-connected injuries. The DVA is not so much derelict in its duty to these injured veterans as it is unsuited to meet their needs. The DVA is a system of health care which is not designed to serve those veterans who are not able to ask for the help they need.

When the DVA rates a disabled ex-POW at 30% or less, as it frequently does, the tendency of these survivors is to accept the rating despite their resentment. For, although the system encourages the veteran to challenge any awards he may deem unjust, few ex-POWs are able to do so. It is not that they are inarticulate or too uneducated. Rather they are governed by the fear that they might lose control of the anger they have bottled up inside themselves and which they have never been able to vent. They are afraid of how they might react should the DVA reject their appeal of a rating decision which they know to be inadequate and unfair.

Suggested Remedies

Restitution

While it is true that the DVA system of compensation is ill-suited to the needs of the ex-POW community, there are other ways to provide for these veterans. One possibility would be an admission by the nations responsible that they have a moral duty to pay compensation to the survivors and their families for the injuries caused by the inhuman treatment they received in those prison camps. The prospects of that happening do not seem bright. The Japanese, for example, who were notorious for their cruel treatment of captives in World War II, never admitted to any wrongdoing.

Standard Disability

The United States could also follow the example of its wartime allies

"I am not complaining or crying, but I have had an awful hard time since the day the war started for all of us on Wake Island. I know everything could have been worse for me over all these years. I am grateful that God has let me live. I am also grateful for all the Veterans Administration has done for me since my discharge from the U.S. Marines in February 1946."
Otis T. Jones
Ocala, Florida

who pay a standard minimum disability compensation to former prisoners of war.[9] Considering the current budget deficit and the peacetime attitudes toward injured veterans, a statutory award is not likely to occur. Because of these circumstances, if there is to be any remedy, it must come through the initiative of the DVA.

New Rating Examinations

What is needed is for the DVA to invite all of the survivors who are able to cooperate – especially those who are being compensated poorly or not at all – to come in for new rating exams. However, this will be an exercise in futility unless the DVA first trains the examiners to understand the peculiar nature of the ex-POWs. The DVA must allow the examiner time to do a proper evaluation, supply the examiner with a medical background of the patient, and allow sufficient time to prepare a thorough report on the results of the examination. If the examiners are to breach the defenses of these survivors, they must appreciate the intense conditioning which governs the behavior of an ex-POW. With patience, determination, and sensitivity, a properly prepared examiner should be able to learn a great deal about the hidden fears, rages, hatreds, and sorrows of these close-mouthed survivors. If that can be accomplished, the DVA will be able to claim a major breakthrough into this relatively untested area of mental health.

DVA Staff: A New Attitude

Let the DVA put out the word to all of its VAMCs that most of the ex-POWs did not volunteer to surrender but were, instead, surrendered by order of their commanding officers. They proved their bravery and their patriotism in bloody combat. A large percentage of them were savagely treated as prisoners and large numbers of their comrades died in prison from that abusive treatment. Those who lived to be repatriated carry with them serious burdens of mind and body which have haunted them ever since.

Let the VAMC personnel learn to view these survivors as the witnesses of suffering and of horrors that few can imagine. If such a new understanding about these injured veterans can come about, perhaps our remaining survivors will begin to look upon the DVA as a friend to be trusted. It is not yet too late for those who are still here.

In Praise of the DVA

The active ex-POWs who are able to make use of the DVA are very grateful for the extra efforts that have been made in the past decade to identify and to deal more effectively with the special needs of the former prisoners of war and their families. Whatever the failings of the DVA in dealing with its ex-POWs during these latter years, it is clearly not due to a lack of caring. This new work has been of great benefit to those survivors and their families who have been well enough to participate in some of these program initiatives.

Let it be understood, therefore, that nothing said here is to be interpreted as a criticism of the DVA. On the contrary, these remarks are made with confidence that the DVA is concerned about its ex-POW population, that it is genuinely interested in improving its services to this group of disabled veterans, and that it welcomes suggestions on how that might be accomplished. The principle problem has been a lack of adequate information about special needs of the former prisoners of war and the reluctance of the members of the ex-POW community to offer such guidance to the DVA. This essay represents the effort of one ex-POW to fill that knowledge gap.

"Most of the doctors I saw had no experience with tropical diseases, could not recognize beriberi or pellagra, knew little about malaria, and absolutely nothing about post traumatic stress disorder. The diagnosis was usually 'The veteran was trying to get a free ride or he was crazy (to a greater or lesser degree)'. I got tired of being treated as though I was a malingerer very early in my contacts with the VA. I certainly did NOT want to have anything in my record about being schizophrenic or paranoiac because I wanted to go to college and get a job — and I was certain that the stigma attached to those conditions would not help me at all. When I found that those diagnoses were being made, I responded in the usual way (the way I'm sure they wanted me to). I said, 'There's not a damned thing wrong with me, brother. I don't need what you are giving me.' And for a long time, I avoided the VA."

John W. Whipple
Tacoma, Washington

Pfc. Robert Brandon rations Red Cross parcel contents, Stalag IX-B.   Courtesy of American Ex-Prisoners of War, Inc.

I Survived, But Was It Worth It?

Isn't it always better to survive than it is to perish? The answer would seem obvious. On the other hand, after almost four years as a prisoner of the Japanese in World War II, and more than 40 years living with the personal aftermath, the question does have some merit. Did we pay too dearly for what we salvaged of our lives?

There are many fates worse than death. Those who face a lifetime of suffering for example, might find that death is a relief. Many of us would rather die than become a burden to our loved ones. Who among us would care to live bed-ridden, incontinent, and unaware of the world around them? A life of abject slavery, or of indeterminant imprisonment with no hope of release would be unbearable to many people. In our prison camps, a common reaction to the death of a comrade was something akin to envy. We would comment that the dead man was fortunate to finally be free, exempt from our future of daily pain, degradation, and humiliation.

I have had occasion to ask myself whether I might have paid too high a price for my survival. This is not the kind of doubt one relates to family members. They can feel offended that their love and devotion have not been enough to make that question superfluous. To all outward appearances, I have had a fairly normal, successful life and I continue to have close and loving relations with my wife and children. Then, why that question?

I do not suffer from terrible guilt for having done something shameful or treacherous to ensure my personal survival at the cost of others' lives. There is nothing in my prison camp history that I would be ashamed to admit. Nor can I recall having engaged in behavior which was despicable in order to save myself from the wrath of my captors. This is not a question of the ends justifying the means. In fact, just the opposite.

I ask myself that question because so much of what I value, so much of what makes life worth living did not survive with me. We survivors are not the men we were before our captivity and we never will be what we might have been. Our experience was so traumatic that it changed us radically in ways that few of us even comprehend. One former prisoner I knew said that he saw his life divided between two different worlds. The period of his life that existed before his capture he remem-

"It is extremely difficult for me to talk or write about my experiences as a POW and how they affect me now. I have felt pain, both physical and emotional, every day for the past 44 years. The intensity varies from moderate to very severe, but it is always there. I have tried to deny its existence for many years, but now I am trying to accept the fact that the pain is real and it is here and to try to do what I can to live with it and ease it some."

John W. Whipple
Tacoma, Washington

39

bers as a time of light, peace, and happiness. Life after capture he sees as dark and unhappy.

Of course, all of us have wondered why fate selected us for survival. It took me many years, however, before I thought to question the value of my survival. It was only after my retirement that I gained enough perspective on my life to feel the true force of that question. When I was younger, driven and overwhelmed with the pressing demands of rearing my children and pursuing a career, I had no time for such introspection.

During those years, I avoided and suppressed all reminders of my imprisonment experiences. But now that I have dropped those barriers and faced up to my background, I have begun to understand how that period of my life has deeply affected me and my family. I can see now the price we prisoners paid for hanging on until liberation.

Liberation itself was a bewildering experience. We did not react to the news with the joyful exuberance you would expect, but with apprehension and confusion at this unexpected reversal of our fortunes. Soon we would return to a world that would be strange and new to us, adjusting to patterns of behavior and family relationships which were no longer familiar.[1]

I do not deny that we were happy to be free. It was just that it took some time for us to grasp what had happened to us. One day we had been expecting to die and the next day we were destined, not only to live, but to return to our homes. It took time for us to accept this as reality and to make the mental change from prisoner to free man. And the adjustment proved more difficult than any of us could imagine – or cared to imagine. To sustain us in those dark days of imprisonment, we made the error of glamorizing our past lives, sanitizing our memories, and glorifying the mundane aspects of life in freedom. We struggled desperately to survive in order to return to that life, only to find it didn't exist. We had set ourselves up for disillusionment and we found it: the realities of personal relations and living conditions could never match our unreal expectations of life after liberation.

We found something else upon our return which was seldom understood by ourselves or others. We found that we were changed, not only physically, because we were more mature, but also in our attitudes and in our perceptions. People and institutions which we had once respected, even revered, lost their ability to impress us. Where once we had been easygoing and accepting, we were now nervous and uncomfortable. Career options that once appealed to us now seemed either unattainable or undesirable. Alcohol became important, providing temporary relief from our anxieties and relieving our nervous tension. Efforts to prepare ourselves academically for professional positions were stymied by our inability to study and an unwillingness to postpone present pleasures for future rewards.

Some of us, like me, were fortunate to marry women who energized us and shielded us with their love through those painful years of adjustment. They gave our lives purpose and meaning. Unfortunately, we could seldom reciprocate their patient love and understanding, responding instead with anger and withdrawal to their efforts to please us.

We can love our wives and children; we can give them loyalty and devotion. But there is some part of us that will always remain detached and apart. This deadening of feeling, which protected us from the pain of witnessing so many deaths, has left us emotional cripples. To compensate, we try to demonstrate feelings by copying the behavior we observe in others. We find ourselves watching others live while we seem only to exist from day to day, untouched and unmoved by the events that should excite us. Some essential human element that gives others joy, sorrow, happiness, and grief has been erased from our natures. We live with the knowledge that it's gone, but without the power to bring it back.

We paid a heavy penalty in staying alive through almost four years of living hell. We did not know then that we would carry the burden of our imprisonment experience with us for the rest of our lives. Nightmares, sleep disturbances, paranoia, and fear will continue to haunt us awake and asleep, for as long as we live. Pain, exhaustion, depression, and irritability follow us wherever we move. The lives we sought to save in prison died within us from the very struggle to stay alive, while the future we imagined has been denied to us.

Was it worth the struggle to live the lives we've been given? I am still asking myself that question. Knowing that the person I was able to save from those death camps is only a poor replica of what I had once been, I wonder if I would do it again. If I had known then what I know now, would I have been able to muster the strength of spirit to avoid so many opportunities to die?

This is a question I cannot answer. Indeed, some part of me feels it is selfish to even ask it. There are those, especially my family, who have benefited from my survival and rejoice that I lived. Perhaps they are the reason I was given the gift of life denied to so many of my comrades. I will never know if I paid too high a price for my life after liberation. But there is a victory, and perhaps a partial answer, in the fact that I can at last raise the question.

"My husband, who served in World War II in the Pacific . . . survived the Death March . . . starved in five prison camps in Japan for 3 1/2 years . . . beaten and brutalized, only to be returned to his family with a broken body and a brain tumor. While he lives today, he is only existing . . . only a frame of a man who needs constant care, . . . constant reassurance 24 hours a day. His insecurities from this horrible 3 1/2 years have not only ruined his life, but mine, as his wife and caregiver . . . his only true friend . . . who lives and relives World War II over and over every day."
Geraldine Meek
Sun City, Arizona

Survivors of the Suchon Tunnel Massacre, Korea. Courtesy of American Ex-Prisoners of War, Inc.

A Wife's View of Her Ex-POW Mate

Since the early 1980s, Dr. Maria Kelnhofer has spoken before groups of former prisoners of war and their spouses, recounting her experiences from more than 40 years of marriage to an ex-POW. In addition to her personal history, Dr. Kelnhofer is qualified to speak on these topics by her medical degree and psychiatric practice; she also holds a masters degree in public health and is near completion on a Ph.D. in psychology. Following is a composite essay taken from the texts of several speeches she has given.

Adjusting to Liberation

I speak to you as a sister who has shared your problems and understands how it feels to love an ex-POW. I also want to lend you some of my expertise as a physician trained to deal with the emotional consequences of living with the stress that comes from marriage to these men. My specialty is psychiatry and I have given considerable attention to the mental problems of former prisoners of war.

My husband was held captive for almost four years by the Japanese in World War II. His captors were as brutal and as vicious as the Nazi storm troopers who played such a large role in the attempted extermination of the Jewish people in Europe. These former prisoners of war are survivors who, by dint of luck and strong constitutions, managed to hang on through illnesses, tortures, starvation, and exhausting labor while their comrades died around them.

The first five years after liberation took an extremely heavy toll on these survivors as they attempted to adjust to their new environment. My husband recalls for me some of the pains of those first few years of liberation. In the fall of 1945, when he was home on repatriation leave, he remembers how he stopped in his tracks, staring in wonder at a man who was cutting his lawn. The lawn cutting, such an ordinary and peaceful civilian activity, struck my husband as utterly bizarre behavior. He had become so adapted to an environment of constant destruction, death, and despair, that a simple routine like cutting the lawn seemed to him an extraordinary event.

When I met Guy in 1947, two years after his liberation, he was hostile, restless, moody, withdrawn, drinking heavily, and subject to frightening nightmares. It was not until 1960, 15 years after his liberation, that

"I had hoped to write before this, but must tell you of our heavy loss. My dear husband, Gene, passed away suddenly October 18, 1986 of a heart attack . . . The government does not allow us much even though our men were rated 100% disabled. They go back to the last rank held, as discharged. Apparently not considering what we as wives endured . . . I have called the POW Hotline, asking for a mental health group for myself, but as yet no help available. Looks like we wives will be forgotten also."
Ann Franklin
Ashland, Wisconsin

my husband was able to stop thinking of himself primarily as an ex-POW. He put it out of his awareness by suppressing his memories, avoiding reminders of that experience, and burying himself in work and family duties.

Until 1985, my husband would not associate with other ex-POWs. When he was diagnosed as 100% disabled as a result of his wartime injuries, he decided, at last, to face down his fear of seeing reminders of that painful past. He began attending group therapy sessions offered to former prisoners of war at the VA hospital in Seattle. Through that experience, he has learned that he is not alone, but that others have shared his experiences and struggles.

Wives of ex-POWs also share a common bond. We are the ones who married these war-battered men. It is we who have borne the burden of caring for them over the years as they wrestled with the physical and psychological consequences of their imprisonment experiences. The pain our husbands have endured in adjusting to life after release has affected the quality of our lives and the lives of our children.

Behavior Traits of the Ex-POW

There is a fairly common behavior pattern which characterizes these former prisoners of war. You and I are keenly aware of these behavior traits, although our husbands often are not. These men are close-mouthed, reticent and, often, hard to approach. They are also socially withdrawn and do not like to be in a crowd or mingle with strangers. You will note that, given the opportunity, they will seat themselves with their backs to a wall where they can observe those who approach them. They are often irritable and impatient, and are unusually sensitive to any demonstration of disrespect. Sleep disturbances are common and nightmares still plunge them back behind prison fences. Depression is chronic with many, and occasional hospitalizations for acute episodes are not uncommon. A large proportion are impotent and many are or have been abusers of alcohol.

Former prisoners of war suffer emotionally as well. They suffer from a kind of psychic numbing that robs them of the common pleasures that life brings to others. Although they have learned to adapt their behavior to conform to social demands, too often they only pretend to feel what those around them truly experience.

Our men were damaged physically and emotionally by the treatment given them in prison camps. But let me point out that they do not suffer these consequences in isolation. Their silences, suspicions, insomnia, and apathy have had their effects on us as well. Put simply, these men are hard to live with. And most wives are not mental health counselors, trained to understand their behavior and discount it.

The Toll on Wives

Caretaking

Too many of us have been blind for too long to the toll that our husbands' prison camp experiences has exacted from us. We did not sit with them behind the barbed wire and the electric fences. We did not endure with them the starvation, the beatings, and the deprivations and humiliations that tried their souls and wracked their bodies. We have, however, borne the agony of watching them suffer through recurring bouts of anger, hatred, remorse, and guilt. We have stood by helplessly while they were tormented with insomnia and nightmares. We have tried unsuccessfully to relieve their restlessness. We have watched their health deteriorate, then nursed and comforted them.

We continue this service now in the final years when our husbands are becoming more handicapped and less able to cope with the legacy of their imprisonment. As their burden increases, so does ours. It would be no exaggeration to say that we too are prisoners, shackled by love and duty because we are so closely bound to these men and have invested so much of our lives in them. We are deeply affected in every way by what happens to them.

Shared Symptoms: Post Traumatic Stress Disorder

It has been my judgment that most of our men suffer from chronic post traumatic stress disorder. Now, PTSD is not contagious like the measles, but you cannot live intimately for many years with one of its victims without becoming a victim yourself. Indeed, some wives have already been hospitalized for symptomatology similar to that of their husbands.[1] How could it be otherwise when you consider how a normal person would be affected by exposure to such behavior? If you live daily for many years with a husband who is often moody, irritable, hard to approach, quick to anger, and socially withdrawn, you are bound to wonder what causes him to behave like that. A natural conclusion is that you have done something, or failed to do something, which has offended him. When he withdraws from you and the children and goes off by himself, you would naturally conclude that he does not like your company or the company of his children. When he cannot sleep or thrashes around at night sweating and shouting in his sleep, he does not tell you what is bothering him; you can't help but feel excluded and that he does not trust you with his troubles.

We see these manifestations of his illness as consequences of some failure on our part. We fight a silent and unknown enemy; he cannot reveal to us that the fault is his, that he suffers from fears and inhibitions tied to a past he cannot share with us.

"Talk about anger. I can well understand why a young person would not want to fight for this country. I feel that my husband's life, the life of my children and my life have been sacrificed for this country and our government has taken care of other countries before administering to the needs of her own veterans. If you have any answers or any suggestions believe me I could surely use them."
Anne L. Massey
Greenville, Mississippi

The wives and children of these disabled former prisoners of war usually know nothing about the prison camp experiences of their husbands and fathers, nor are they likely to hear about it from them. These men are not being secretive when they fail to reveal these details of their past, nor is it entirely an effort to shield us from harm. For the most part, the subject is out of bounds for everyone, except those who shared the experience with them. They are doing what comes naturally to someone with PTSD; they are coping with their painful memories by suppressing them.[2] My husband tried one time to tell me about the way the Japanese had treated them, but he broke down and cried, unable to share those memories with me. This takes its toll. When the wife and children are living with a man whose behavior they can only interpret in their own terms, they blame themselves for their inability to please him and win his affection.

Broken Marriages

And how have we been affected by living out our lives with men who behave as I have described? What has been the impact on us of trying to manage a household, rear a family, and have a little fun in our lives?

Fortunately for myself, I have no regrets and my husband and I have managed to develop and maintain a long-lasting relationship of love and respect. Others have not been so lucky. For some, the marriage survives, but with a burden of hurts and disappointments that seriously damages the relationship. A few have made alcohol, drugs, and extramarital sex their escape valves. And we find some of our sisters in the mental health wards at the hospital, overcome with depression because it became too much for them. The women who did leave their marriages did it to save themselves. They found they just could not continue the fight to keep love and caring alive.[3]

Anger

There is one response to this stress which is common to all of us: a tremendous reservoir of anger. We are angry because these men behave in ways we consider hurtful and thoughtless, and because of the way they treat our family and friends. We are angry because they do not notice the efforts we make to cheer them up, to make them more comfortable and to make ourselves more attractive to them. And we are angry because they are more of a burden to us now when we too are becoming tired. We would like for ourselves more of the personal attention and care that their failing health demands from us. We are angry especially because we do not feel appreciated and loved for all the sacrifices we have made for them.

Wives and children who are deeply offended at the way they are treated by their ex-POW husbands and fathers learn to hide that anger from these irritable and unpredictable men. They learn to mask that anger even from themselves. Fear is one factor that leads to suppressing anger. But the ex-POW can also be someone who demonstrates in many ways that he is a loving and responsible husband and father. Nor does it seem proper to be angry with a former prisoner of war, because he has suffered enough and he is obviously not fully recovered from his injuries. Although they are rightfully angry on many occasions because of the behavior of the ex-POW, wives and children often do not admit to themselves that this inner bundle of anger exists. Like the ex-POW, they never express their anger, never release or vent it.

What happens to the anger that the wives and children of the ex-POWs keep hidden and secret? Does undemonstrated, unsatisfied anger just dissipate, leaving no residue to show that it ever existed?

We must understand that we have a right to be angry. If we try to pretend that we are not angry, we are denying our humanity. When we try to hide from ourselves these natural human emotions, we are likely to find that our bodies will not accept such misrepresentations. We will find that we are often nervous, depressed, sleepless, and irritable. Drugs and alcohol can then become the substitutes for venting the anger we are suppressing.

Using Anger for Change

I want to suggest that we deal with that anger in constructive ways. First, we must learn to live more normally and productively, despite our hidden burdens. One way to do this is to join together with other spouses of former prisoners of war. The VA medical center near your home is prepared to help by providing space and the services of a trained therapist to assist in directing your meetings. These therapy groups are a wonderful source of emotional support. You are in the company of those who know what you know and who have faced the same daily pressures.[4]

Another healthy way to use that anger is to defuse it by attacking one of its major sources: the terrible inequities and failures of our government system in meeting the needs of our disabled veterans and their families. These are not immutable laws; they are the direct (correctable) results of the efforts of men and women such as ourselves to solve problems through the political process. We can make it better for ourselves and for those who follow if we care enough and are angry enough to enact better laws and more humane and workable regulations.

We need to use our anger also in becoming more active and better informed about the needs of those who cannot help themselves. Let us see to it that our husbands have their protocol exam. When he dies, let us be sure we demand an autopsy. Let us unite as wives in every chap-

"Never pity, only a sadness underlies my daily existence with my husband, as I ponder the way our lives have been lived over these past decades. Sometimes I rebel – I feel devastated – because I cannot change my husband's life and put back a whole man as he was meant to be."

Geraldine Meek
Sun City, Arizona

ter of our ex-POW organizations to develop legislative remedies to our common problems so that we are not left destitute and unrewarded for the role we have played in caring for this country's disabled veterans.[5]

If these things are to be done, they must be done by us, the wives. Our men do not have the strength any more to undertake such a struggle and see it through. They do not, in most cases, recognize or admit that they are disabled. We wives know that these men are sick. We know because we live with them and we interact with them intimately on a daily basis. Maybe they can fool the doctors at the DVA, but they cannot fool us. Maybe they can even fool themselves into believing that all is well with them, but we know better.

What is more, we know that their behavior, however unaware of it they may be, has wounded us. Perhaps the government should have warned all of us impressionable young ladies – who thought these men would make good husbands and fathers – of the health risks of marrying ex-POWs.

Forgiving: Our Husbands, Ourselves

After enduring so much for so long, many of us, like our husbands, have become apathetic. I have heard such responses as "It's too late now," and "Where were you 40 years ago?" Is it really too late? If you want to understand what has happened and why, it is not too late. It may be possible, through this new understanding, to get a better perspective on the past and to be more forgiving, if not of him, then of yourself.

I am suggesting that you begin to forgive yourselves for being human. For having tried and for having done all you were capable of doing and finding it was not enough. Begin to focus on all the good will you invested in your marriages, on all the efforts you made to create a happy and loving home environment, and give yourself credit for all the good you accomplished under very trying circumstances.

Overall, we have done a fantastic job. Let us be aware, as many of our husbands are now beginning to understand, that without us, these men would not have made it at all. Take comfort in the knowledge that these men survived the painful and difficult conversion from prisoners of war to husbands, fathers, wage-earners and productive, taxpaying citizens, because we rescued them. It was our love, attention, caring, and support that allowed these men to make it back to the real world. I beg you not to be too hard on yourselves.

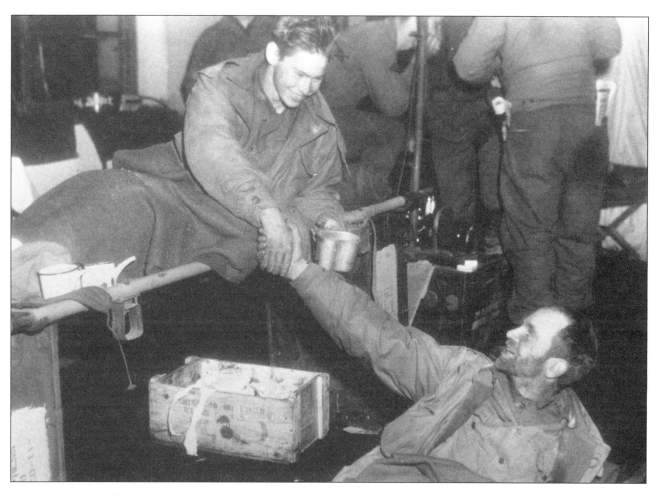

Private Robert Collins and M/Sgt. Woodrow Haines back behind UN lines, Chechon, Korea. Courtesy of American Ex-Prisoners of War, Inc.

Group Therapy and The Ex-POW

1985 was the year I decided to break out of my self-imposed isolation and begin to associate for the first time with other ex-POWs. To my surprise I found that there was a group of former prisoners of war meeting regularly at the VA Hospital in Seattle. I joined the group and met with them on a weekly basis for the whole year that I lived in that city. It was an experience which I found so rewarding that I wish to recommend it to others who, like me, have feared the consequences of such an encounter with other former prisoners of war.

The group in Seattle had a membership of 25 to 30 men who had been coming together for more than three years. A psychotherapist appointed by the VA acted as the leader of the group. The meetings I attended were unstructured, informal affairs in which the men talked freely about their different experiences in coping with life's demands. People talked about their jobs, their families, their hobbies, their daily lives as they saw them affected by their prison camp experiences. No one used this forum to dredge up gory details about the tortures and humiliations they had endured as prisoners of war.

Some people might think anyone coming to such therapy sessions must be unable to cope, or seriously disturbed. To the contrary, most of those who appeared regularly in our group were sober, quiet, neatly dressed, polite, and attentive. Nothing in their outward appearance or their behavior would distinguish them from the crowd. Yet, all of those who came regularly demonstrated that they had the classic symptoms of chronic post traumatic stress disorder: trouble controlling their tempers, sleep disturbances, sexual dysfunctions, bouts of depression, difficult communications with spouses and family members, restlessness and frequent moves, inability to form strong emotional attachments, a tendency to cry at inappropriate moments, and avoidance of reminders of their imprisonment. I believe they were a typical group of ex-POWs.

Without exception, the members in the group reported that their participation in these sessions was very helpful to them. Some of them said that they were sleeping better, and that they felt more at ease with themselves since attending the meetings. Most acknowledged that this

"I have been going to the Mental Hygiene Clinic for group meetings now for about 10 or 12 years at the VA hospital in Gainesville, Florida. These group meetings have helped me in a lot of ways. I think I can cope with a lot more things now, than I could before I went to these group meetings."
Otis T. Jones
Ocala, Florida

was a unique outlet because it was the only place where they could speak freely about matters which others would not understand or believe.

Not everyone who came to the group meetings spoke out. Some members who came regularly said little or nothing although they listened intently to what others said. Some were not able to overcome their fear of breaking down in front of others and they held their silence for that reason. It was not uncommon for men to be overcome with emotion, and tears were accepted as the natural consequences of many of the things that were said. On rare occasions the men became angry with one another or took offense at some remark made by the therapist. Then some of the men who were sensitive to conflicts in the group would withdraw until the atmosphere calmed down.

One great benefit from participation in these group sessions is that the veteran realizes that his personal problems are not unique. He finds that many other ex-POWs behave as he does and that they suffer from the same kinds of difficulties in their daily lives. Instead of wondering whether he is cracking up, he finds that his fears and depressions are quite normal for people with his kind of prison background. While he may recognize that his own life has been adversely affected by what happened to him in prison camps, he will often find others in the group who have been more severely damaged and who are less able than he to cope with life's daily stresses. From all this he will get a clearer appreciation of the common conditions uniting ex-POWs.[1]

"I believe that more could have been done for the returning POWs, more understanding and recognition of their great sacrifice. Being a prisoner of war was an experience he seemed to want to keep hidden away because it made him different. Few of our friends ever knew of it, even in the military. When I persuaded him to join the ex-POWs just a few years ago, it was of great benefit to him. He even met a former cellmate and the release of all those feelings between the men was wonderful to watch. They could talk and understand one another."
Leona M. Dye
Olympia, Washington

I know that there are many more ex-POWs out there who need to break out of the barriers they have erected between themselves and the rest of the population of former prisoners of war. I would urge them to come in to their VA hospitals to join with men of similar backgrounds to talk out their common concerns and to learn from them more about themselves. Because I too hid out, I know what they fear. For my part, I found the fears, if not groundless, were at least greatly exaggerated in my mind. The benefits, on the other hand, were much greater than I had imagined they would be. I hope many more of our comrades will brave their fears and take a chance, understanding that it is not a commitment and they are always free to withdraw if it proves to be more than they can handle.

Nichols Field Detail, P.I., taken at Pasay schoolhouse.

The POW Medal: What it Means

Receiving a medal for military service should be a proud moment, an event signifying a nation's gratitude for a job well done. Why, then, did I feel so disappointed by the Prisoner of War Medal? I had certainly earned it, and the recognition was long overdue. No one expected the medal to compensate for our suffering; on the other hand, a little respect with the medal would have gone a long way toward that goal.

In 1988, I received in the mail a new military decoration, the Prisoner of War Medal. My eligibility for the award was earned by my years as a prisoner of the Japanese during World War II. The medal was received with mixed emotions by me and by my comrades in arms.

In one sense, I was offended by the medal. It was so belated, coming as it did more than 40 years after my liberation from prison camp. Moreover, it was such an inadequate recognition, representing the only official acknowledgement we have ever been accorded for the suffering we endured for our country. The manner of its presentation left a great deal to be desired. How much significance can be given to a decoration that is sent to the recipient in the mail without the minimal courtesy of an accompanying letter of explanation or gratitude? Where is the honor in that?

"After 43 years, my husband has just now had mailed to him a POW Medal. Over a year ago he was mailed a Bronze Star Medal. How very cold, after 43 years, to receive this recognition through the mail. How militarily rude, to present a medal in this manner. I have seen on television a number of times, the President giving personal accolades to less deserving, less accomplished people than those who performed with dignity for their country when they gave of their lives."

Geraldine Meek
Sun City, Arizona

The medal lost some of its luster, too, by the unfriendly reception it was given by some members of the military community. In their ignorance, they complained that men were being honored not for fighting but for giving up. This kind of condemnation by misinformed critics has cast a cloud on the award. Unfortunately, these protestations also reflect a widespread misconception about the prisoner of war experience.

The Prisoner of War Medal is given to those members of the armed forces who exhibited unusual courage and steadfastness during prolonged periods of extreme stress and maximum danger while in the hands of the enemy. Despite years of torture, starvation, beatings, humiliations, and slave labor, these men and women conducted themselves so as to preserve and defend the honor and integrity of the United States. Their unswerving loyalty, discipline and patriotism remained intact under the most trying conditions to which the human mind and body can be subjected.

Unlike the benign conditions portrayed in movie versions of life in prison camps, the prisoner of war was usually treated brutally by his captors. Upon release, there were no parades, no ceremonies of homecoming, and no attention to the serious aftereffects of imprisonment experiences. It is time for this nation to acknowledge with this small token its debt to those who gave so much in defense of their country. The Prisoner of War Medal deserves respect from the military family.

Three American POWs released by the Viet Cong near Tay Ninh City.   Courtesy of American Ex-Prisoners of War, Inc.

APPENDIX 1
What It Was Like: Prison Camp
Experiences as Told by the Survivors

GORDON NELSON

Gordon Nelson of Sun Lakes, Arizona, from a talk given at the "Former Prisoner of War Educational Conference: Medical and Psychosocial Issues," December 2-4, 1986, at the Northeast Regional Medical Center, Middleville Road, Northport, New York.

I was on the infamous Bataan Death March of over 80 miles in four days without food or water in the tropical sun of the Philippines. We had been held three days in the jungle before the march began, during which time we had no food and very little water. Prior to our being surrendered all of our supplies were nearly exhausted. We had existed for over two months on a small portion of rice twice a day and what we could scrounge from the jungle. Ninety-five percent of our troops had malaria, dysentery, and jungle diseases, and the effects of malnutrition were already visible. Many medical supplies were exhausted. Well over 1,000 Americans died on the Death March and 9,000 made it to Camp O'Donnell where over 1,500 died in the next few weeks.

During the next 3 1/2 years, I was in six prison camps in the Philippines, 17 days in the hold of a cargo ship to Japan, and in three prison camps in Japan. Our food was mostly what had been rejected by the Japanese military. It was mildewed, rancid, weevil-infested, and often only partially cooked. We supposedly had 800 calories a day on which to work 10 or 13 hours.

During the 3 1/2 years, I had bacillary dysentery, amoebic dysentery, yellow jaundice, malaria, dengue fever, scurvy, pellegra, beriberi, pneumonia (twice), malnutritional skin ulcerations, lice, and, in Japan over a three-week period, my feet and hands were severely frostbitten. It was severe enough that dead skin peeled in spots to the bone on my two thumbs and forefingers. In addition, I was subjected to over a hundred beatings or tortures. For over three years I weighed less than 103 pounds and at one point I was down to 75 pounds. Yet I was on work detail 90% of the time. If one didn't work, their rations were cut in half.

At the Cabanatuan Prison Camp, where we were sent after Camp O'Donnell, we carved a 500-acre vegetable farm out of a swamp infested with ants and cobras. While chopping down anthills, six to eight feet tall, we fought over the cobras that lived there. They were prized for food, along with any protein we could find. The farm was for the Japanese military and we were often beaten for stealing vegetables. One day the guards had us load a 12x16 foot litter with wet Chinese cabbage. It later weighed in over 600 pounds. Eight prisoners were forced to lift it and then the four in the middle were beaten off, leaving four of us to carry it. The man on my right at the rear of the litter passed out just as a guard hit me in the small of the back with the butt of his rifle. I passed out and was carried into camp. I was not able to get up and walk for the next three weeks. I worked the rest of my prison days with severe back pains. Upon returning home, the VA issued me a steel and leather back brace which I wore, off and on, for the next 14 years. I still have back problems.

From Cabanatuan I was sent to Lepa where an airport was being constructed. Shortly after arrival the steamroller broke down. Over 400 of us were forced to march, stamping heel to toe, from dawn till dark, for over three weeks to pack a runway. Then I came down with pneumonia and was transferred to the Bilibid Prison in Manila.

In Japan, they used 600 of us to power a pile driver. With 200 prisoners on each of three ropes, we took turns lifting and dropping the weight from a tall tripod. The rope burns we got were nasty, but we drove a lot of piling.

In Japan, I also worked in a coal mine three-fourths of a mile underground where the only air was from a power hose for operating the drill and jack-hammer. When one of us passed out, the guard would disconnect the hose to give us air and slap the one who was unconscious until he came around. I purposely broke my foot to get out of that mine. The guard wanted to shoot me, claiming I had done it on purpose, but the mine supervisor prevailed and I was given a pick handle for a cane to walk out of the mine. For the next several weeks, until I was transferred out of that camp, I had to report to the Camp Commandant every morning along with others who could not work. Every morning he would call me "uncareless" and knock me down, expecting me to get back up at attention, often to be knocked down again. Six weeks later, in another camp, they operated through the sole of my foot to remove bone splinters – without anesthesia!

Later at that Fukuoka Camp, three of us were caught stealing water at our noon break. The head of the guard ordered the three of us beaten. We were taken to the guardhouse where the guards intermittently took turns beating us over the heads with large bamboo poles all afternoon. At the end of the work day, the three of us were taken to a large clearing where the other prisoners were already assembled in a large circle. In the center of that circle, the head of the guard told us to do pushups, "First man down dies!" The head of the guard would work on one of us to be sure we were doing the pushups properly while the other two rested. After about an hour of that game, one of my buddies passed out and was bayoneted through the back until dead.

In the Cabanatuan Camp I had a severe head infection with my face so swollen I could hardly see out of my eyes. While there was very little medicine in camp, they did try to keep us in condition to work. They sprayed 10% cocaine up both nostrils morning and night for a couple of months. I must admit it was my happiest time in prison camp. The swelling went down about the time I was shipped to Japan in a cargo ship. Nine hundred of us were in one hold of the ship and didn't get up on deck for the whole 17-day trip. There was not room to lie down, which was just as well as there were no toilet facilities and the floor was like a barnyard.

But my lowest point was in the Cabanatuan Camp when I had severe dysentery and came down with yellow jaundice (hepatitis). One of the American doctors in camp could only suggest that I try to find some sugar and take a tablespoon several times a day to keep my liver functioning, even though it would make my dysentery worse. For three days I searched that camp of 13,000 men for sugar. I finally found a prisoner who had been driving truck for the Japanese and had smuggled a small sack back to camp. After much haggling I finally bought nine cups for $45 I had received from a gold watch I had smuggled through the Death March.

By this time I was so bloated and stinking I was unfit to be in the barracks. I crawled out near the latrine because I needed to be there. In a few days I was so weak I couldn't get up from where I lay. When it rained, the latrines overflowed and I lay in filth and maggots. My feet and legs ulcerated and were infested with maggots. The guards wanted to have me buried on several occasions but my buddies, who brought me water every day, convinced them I was living. No one survived prison camp without the help of friends. By some miracle, I crawled away from that spot over four weeks later, weighing perhaps 70 pounds. Mine was not an isolated case. I have seen over 100 prisoners at one time or another lying alone on the ground, more dead than alive, but some of the lucky ones survived.

Shortly after I got back in the barracks, an old man who had also been a prisoner in Egypt during World War I gave me some of his "cure" for dysentery. It was potassium permanganate crystals, a disinfectant used in gymnasium foot baths. He explained it was poison but, if I began with a minute quantity and increased it I could build up a tolerance. It seemed to help. Then a buddy, working on the wood detail in a swamp, brought me in several duck eggs which I hard-boiled. In a couple weeks I regained some strength and I, too, was on the wood detail.

* * *

I believe it was those weeks of laying on that filthy ground that caused me later to have one of the medical mysteries of ex-POWs. For the next 39 years I had a syndrome of itchy skin welts, abdominal pains, and lung congestion. The itchy welts would appear over many areas of my body. They came on suddenly, two to four inches long, looking like worms under the inflamed skin. Attacks might last from only a few hours to several days, but there were very few months in the 39 years that I didn't have one or more attacks. Often, due to the itching, I could not sleep. During those years, I saw 28 or 30 specialists. I was diagnosed for hives, nerves, food allergies, respiratory allergies, chronic bronchitis, digestive disorders, and suspected parasites, though numerous stool specimens were always negative. I was put through extensive tests, treatment plans, and medications. Nothing helped or gave me any relief. Most of the specialists were not VA doctors as I had very little contact with the VA from 1960 to 1981. I became very, very frustrated!

In January 1982, I was placed on a steroid medication for arthritis in the hands and feet. My itchy welts flared up far worse than ever before and my lungs and bronchial tubes got very congested with phlegm.

Miraculously, I ran across an article on Strongyloidiasis in the Med-Search column of the *Ex-POW Bulletin*. The article explained that Strongyloides are a self-perpetuating parasite with the larvae circulating from the intestines to the lungs and also crawling under the skin causing hive-like eruptions that are very itchy. The parasite can also attack other body organs, even the brain, causing Strongyloides Encephalitis. If the body's defense mechanism breaks down, usually associated with malnutrition, steroids, or cancer treatments, a hyperinfection often results in death. It mentioned that the only effective treatment is thiabendazole, perfected by the British in 1967. The article was very thorough. I immediately discontinued the steroid medication I had taken for six weeks.

I immediately phoned Stan Sommers who heads POW MedSearch supported by the American Ex-POWs, Inc. He referred me to Otto Schwarz who did their work on Strongyloides. He told me that he had had Strongyloidiasis that was undiagnosed until he took a trip to Australia where veterans had been treated for the condition. He said that after the British had perfected the thiabendazole in 1967 they had screened their Far East ex-POWs and treated them at the College of Tropical Medicine in Liverpool. Australia and Canada had followed up. He said he had returned and worked hard to get a VA program started. In 1980, he finally succeeded with Dr. Pelletier in heading a research program on Strongyloides at the American Lake VA in Tacoma, Washington. He gave me Dr. Pelletier's phone number.

I phoned Dr. Pelletier, but was informed by his secretary that I should go to my local VA as their research was limited to the "Bridge over the

River Kwai" prison camp ex-POWs, where Strongyloides were known to be prevalent. I went to the Phoenix VA hospital where the doctor told me if I thought I had parasites crawling under my skin he would refer me to a psychiatrist. Refusing to look at the research papers I had brought, he did look at my skin welts and referred me to a dermatologist. The dermatologist did listen, but then checked with the pharmacy only to be told they did not carry thiabendazole. So mebendazole was prescribed and stool specimens ordered. They were negative. I took the medication without results.

My condition was getting worse. I had 14 welts from shoulder to waist on one side of my body and on numerous other places. I was coughing phlegm constantly, couldn't sleep, and was almost losing bowel control from diarrhea. I continued to call Dr. Pelletier's office at American Lake VA and made a pest of myself, but never got through to the doctor. Meanwhile, Otto Schwarz had sent me a large packet of research which I took to a private doctor. He could not get a positive stool from his lab, but finally became convinced that I did have Strongyloidiasis and ordered out thiabendazole from a pharmaceutical firm. It took over 10 days to arrive.

Unexpectedly, the next day I received a mail stool specimen kit from American Lake VA. Four days after I mailed in the first specimen I received a phone call from Dr. Pelletier confirming that I had Strongyloides Stercoralis. The medicine ordered by my private doctor finally came and I took the course with a repeat one week later. The treatment was severe but the results were dramatic. For the first time in 39 years, I finally had relief.

Diagnosis of Strongyloides by stool specimen is very difficult. Quoting from Dr. Pelletier, on those cases that have tested positive "fifteen coverslips per stool were examined. Fifty percent of the positive cases were found after 1.7 hours of microscopy, 90% after five hours, and 100% after 10 hours of microscopy." It is rare that a lab examines that extensively. Dr. Pelletier's funding ran out at American Lake VA. He transferred to the Wichita VA and was re-funded, but he had lost his lab staff. I was followed up after two years from Wichita. The last I heard, funding had run out.

* * *

Upon discharge from the army in 1946, I enrolled in the University of Minnesota Law School. Before mid-quarter I had passed out on the campus and was admitted to the University Hospital. They found a duodenal and 17 intestinal ulcers and advised surgery to remove 19 feet of my intestines. I refused and after four more consultations, I still refused. So I was referred to a psychiatrist and a dietitian. I was placed on a very limited diet and lost weight again. I hadn't returned from being a POW to be hungry all the time. I finally found a doctor who understood the origins of my problems in malnutrition and got me back to eating almost everything. I regained my normal weight and, though I have since had to endure a spastic colon, that is much better than little or no colon or all.

I also have sprue and must take B-12 shots every month due to a problem of digestive malabsorption. I am on medication for circulatory disorder and high blood pressure, as well as periodic anxiety and depression. I lost all my teeth due to scurvy damage to the gums. I have had to live with nightmares of torture, so I do not sleep well. During the period I was going to private doctors, I was diagnosed on three occasions by separate clinics as having a marked endocrine imbalance and was on hormone shots, off and on, for a total of seven years. I also had an artery break, post-nasal, in 1974 and again in 1976, after which I requested demotions in my job because of hypertension. I also had plastic surgery on my upper eyelids, which had puffed up so bad it was an effort to keep my eyes open.

In 1980, I began to have severe dizzy spells with triple vision and brilliant auras. I had extensive testing, including brain scans but no positive diagnosis was made. Without diagnosis I could not get disability retirement, so I took voluntary retirement in 1981 at the age of 61. But I had had a very successful career in the field of juvenile delinquency and detention. I had learned from being a POW how people should not be treated. I fought against group punishment and physical abuse in juvenile institutions and tried to keep dependent, neglected, and runaway children out of delinquency institutions. I was administrator of juvenile detention for over nine years and national consultant in the children's bureau of the old Department of Health, Education and Welfare in Washington for five years. I was a workaholic and, at times, near being an alcoholic. They were a means of escape from ruminating.

I thank my heritage that I have a strong constitution! Yet, I have lived in a gray world since POW days. I learned early that I cannot discuss my POW experiences socially without alienating people. I learned to respect my wife when she says "shush!" Most ex-POWs cannot talk about their experiences, which are repressed and fester in their subconscious mind. But the vast majority of them need someone who can empathize with their anxieties, depressions, nightmares, suicidal wishes, and a vast array of physical problems too often misunderstood. I speak for all ex-POWs, whether they were held in Vietnam, Korea, Germany, or Japan. We all share the pain. The families of ex-POWs have also shared in that pain, especially the wives and children. Living with an ex-POW is not easy.

IRVING SILVERLIEB

From a letter to the Veterans Administration. Mr. Silverlieb resides in St. Louis Park, Minnesota.

I have a great fear of having to become dependent on other people, fear of strokes, or other crippling disease. I have a very hard time trying to become close to people, even my own family. I find it very hard to hug my own wife, children, or grandchildren. I will shake hands instead. When my children ask me about this problem, my answer is, I lost too many friends as a POW and I don't want to be hurt anymore.

When my children and grandchildren were small I couldn't stand to hear them cry, remembering the Japanese torturing children to get us mad so we would react and they could kill us.

I keep thinking about the time the Japanese came down to the hold of the ship we were on. They picked five guys at random – one of the guys was standing next to me – and took all of them to the topside of the ship and beheaded them. This was a warning to us to not cause any trouble. I also remember a buddy getting bayoneted by the guard because the guard thought my friend had a smile on his face. I keep remembering missing meal after meal as a group punishment. I was near death because I contracted malaria, beriberi, pellagra, and other diseases. By the time the war ended, I weighed 90 pounds.

I often think about when we left Korea in a 21-ship convoy and 11 of those ships were sunk. I dream about being back in the coal mines 2,000 feet underground, 3,000 feet away from the shaft in half-flooded mines, standing in freezing water for 10 hours a day. I dream about seeing a guy beaten because the guards did not think we were doing enough.

*   *   *

My family and friends tell me that I am getting too heavy and putting on a lot of weight. Well, I'd rather be fat and happy than hungry and thin. I like new jewelry and watches. They tell me I spend too much on them. I believe this is my money and I can spend it any way I want.

One bad thing about being retired is that I am thinking more and more about my days as a POW. I am even starting to drink too much again and I am having more nightmares.

It is very seldom that I argue. As a POW I learned to know that it would be very dangerous to argue and that to stay alive I had to walk away. The Japanese treated me as if I was not a person. Our own American doctors treated all of the POWs worse than the Japanese [treated us]. The Japanese inflicted physical pain, the American doctors inflicted mental pain. I was made to feel like I was a mental case. Most ex-POWs have avoided the VA and American doctors because they did not understand post traumatic stress syndrome.

When I would tell the doctors of my fears and dreams, they told me not to worry, everyone has these same fears. (I'm talking about snakes, seeing snakes crawl out of mass Chinese graves.) Nightmares about being killed or maimed by our own planes or ships. I dream of being threatened with death because of other people's behavior.

DR. LESLIE CAPLAN

Dr. Leslie Caplan, a flight surgeon on a mission out of Italy, was captured in Yugoslavia in October 1944 when his B-24 was shot down. He was sent to Pomerania as a prisoner of war and soon found himself the only physician on a forced march of 2,500 allied POWs over 600 miles. Following is part of Dr. Caplan's sworn testimony about the conditions of the march, given to the Civil Affairs Division of the War Crimes Office, December 31, 1947.

Q. State what you know concerning the mistreatment of American Prisoners of War at Stalag Luft #4.

A. The camp was opened about April, 1944, and was an Air Force Camp. It was located at the Gross Tyshow about two miles from the Kief Heide railroad station. In the summer of 1944 the Russian offensive threatened Stalag Luft #6, so approximately 1,000 Americans were placed on a ship for evacuation to Stalag Luft #4. Upon arrival at the railroad station, certain groups were forced to run the two miles to Stalag Luft #4 at the points of bayonets. Those who dropped behind were either bayoneted or were bitten on the legs by police dogs.

Q. Were these wounds serious enough to cause any deaths?

A. All were flesh wounds and no deaths were caused by the bayoneting.

Q. Did you see these men at the time of the bayoneting?

A. No. This happened prior to my arrival at Luft #4.

Q. Did you see any of the men who were bitten by dogs?

A. Yes, I personally saw the healed wounds on the legs of a fellow named Smith or Jones (I am not certain as to the name) who had been severely bitten. There were approximately 50 bites on each leg. It looked as though his legs had been hit with small buckshots. This man remained an invalid confined to his bed all the time I was at Luft #4.

Q. Do you know how many men were injured as a result of the bayonet runs?

A. I was told that about 20 men had been hospitalized as a result. Many other bayoneted men were not hospitalized due to limited medical facilities.

Q. Do you know if the Commandant was responsible for the bayoneting and dog bites?

A. I did not know the Commandant and I do not know who was responsible. Captain Pickhardt, the officer in charge of the guards, is said to have incited the guards by telling them that American Airmen were gangsters who received a bonus for bombing German children and women. Most of the guards were older men and fairly reasonable, but other guards were pretty rough. "Big Stoop" was the most hated of the guards.

Q. For what reason was "Big Stoop" disliked?

A. He beat up on many of our men. He would cuff the men on the ears with an open-handed sideway movement. This would cause pressure on the eardrums which sometimes punctured them.

Q. Could you give any specific incidents of such mistreatment by "Big Stoop"?

A. Yes, I treated some of the men whose eardrums had been ruptured by the cuffing administered by "Big Stoop".

Q. State what you know concerning the forced march from Stalag Luft #4.

A. In February, 1945, the Russian Offensive threatened to engulf Stalag Luft #4. On 6 February, 1945, about 6,000 prisoners were ordered to leave the camp on foot after only a few hours notice. We left in three separate sections, A, C, and D. I marched with Section C which had approximately 2,500 men. It was a march of great hardship. For 53 days we marched long distances in bitter weather and on starvation rations. We lived in filth and slept in open fields or barns. Clothing, medical facilities and sanitary facilities were utterly inadequate. Hundreds of men suffered from malnutrition, exposure, tuberculosis, and other diseases. No doubt many men are still suffering today as a result of that ordeal.

Q. How much food was issued to the men of this march?

A. According to my records, during the 53 days of the march, the Germans issued us rations which I have since figured out contained a total of 770 calories per day. The German ration was mostly in potatoes and contained very little protein. [Food from other sources over] the same 53-day period averaged 566 calories per day. This means that our caloric intake per day on the march amounted to 1,336 calories.

This is far less than the minimum required to maintain body weight, even without the strenuous physical activity we were compelled to undergo in the long marches.

The area we marched through was rural and there were no food shortages there. We slept in barns and often saw large supplies of potatoes which we could not get at. We all felt that the German officers in our column could have obtained more supplies for us. They contended that the food we saw was needed elsewhere. They further contended that the reason we received so little Red Cross supplies was that the Allied Air Force (of which we were "Gangster members") had disrupted the German transportation that carried Red Cross supplies. This argument was disproved later when we continued our march under the jurisdiction of another prison camp; namely Stalag #2B. This was during the last month of the war when German transportation was at its worst. Even so, we received a good ration of potatoes almost daily and received frequent issues of Red Cross food, far more than we were given under the jurisdiction of Stalag Luft #4.

Q. What sort of shelter was provided during the 53-day march?

A. Mostly we slept in barns. We were usually herded into these barns so closely that it was impossible for all men to find room to lie down. It was not unusual for many men to stand all night or to be compelled to sleep outside because there was no room inside. Usually there was some straw for some of us to lie on, but many had to lie in barn filth or in dampness. Very frequently there were large parts of the barn (usually drier and with more straw) that were denied to us. There seemed to be no good reason why we should have to sleep in barnyard filth or stand in a crowded barn while other sections of the barn were not used. The Germans sometimes gave no reason for this, but at other times, it was made clear to us that if we slept in the clean straw its value to the animals would be less because we would make it dirty. At other times barns were denied us because the Germans stated having PW's in the barn might cause a fire that would endanger livestock.

It was very obvious that the welfare of German cattle was placed above our welfare. On February 14, 1945, Section C of Stalag Luft #4 had marched approximately 35 kilometers. There were many stragglers and sick men who could barely keep up. That night the entire column slept in a cleared area in the woods near Schweinemunde. It had rained a good bit of the day and the ground was soggy, but it froze before morning. We had no shelter whatever and were not allowed to forage for firewood. The ground we slept on was littered by the feces of dysenteric prisoners who had stayed there previously. There were many barns in the vicinity, but no effort was made to accommodate us there. There were hundreds of sick men in the column that night. I slept with one that was suffering from pneumonia.

Q. What were the conditions on this march as regards to drinking water?

A. Very poor. Our sources of water were unsanitary surface water and well water often of questionable sanitary quality. At times so little water was issued to us that men drank wherever they could. While there was snow on the ground, it was common for the men to eat snow whether it was dirty or not. At other times, men drank from ditches that others had used as latrines. I personally protested these conditions many times. The German doctor from Stalag Luft #4 (Capt. Sommers or Sonners) agreed that the lack of sanitary water was the principal factor responsible for the dysentery that plagued our men. It would have been a simple matter to issue large amounts of boiled water which would have been safe regardless of its source. At times we were issued adequate amounts of boiled water but at other times, not enough safe water was available.We often appealed to be allowed to collect fire-wood and boil water ourselves in the many boilers that were standard equipment on almost every German farm. This appeal was granted irregularly. When it was granted, the men lined up in the cold for hours to await the tedious distribution. Another factor that forced an unnecessary [hardship] on us was that when we first left Stalag Luft #4, the men were not permitted to take along a drinking utensil. The first few issues of boiled water were, therefore, not widely distributed for there were no containers for the men to collect the water in. As time went on, each man collected a tin can from the Red Cross food supplies and this filthy container was the sole means of collecting water or the soup that sometimes was issued to us.

Q. What medical facilities were available on the march from Stalag Luft #4?

A. They were pitiful. From the very start large numbers of men began to fall behind. Blisters became infected and many men collapsed from hunger, fear, malnutrition, exhaustion, or disease. We organized groups of men to aid the hundreds of stragglers. It was common for men to drag themselves along in spite of intense suffering. Many men marched along with large abscesses on their feet or frostbite of extremities. Many others marched with temperatures as high as 105 degrees. I personally slept with men suffering from Eyrsipelas, diphtheria, pneumonia, malaria, dysentery, and other diseases. The most common was dysentery for this was an inevitable consequence of the filth we lived in and the unsanitary water we drank. This was so common and so severe that all ordinary rules of decency were meaningless. Hundreds of men on this march suffered so severely from dysentery that they lost control of their bowel movements because of severe cramps, and soiled themselves. Wherever our column went, there was a trail of bloody movements and discarded underwear (which was sorely needed for warmth).

At times the Germans gave us a few small farm wagons to carry our sick. The most these wagons ever accommodated was 35 men but we had hundreds of men on the verge of collapse. It was our practice to load the wagon. As a man would collapse he would be put on the wagon and some sick man on the wagon would be taken off to make way for his exhausted comrade. When our column would near a permanent PW camp we were allowed to send our sickest men there while the rest of our column marched on. We were never allowed to leave all of our sick. I do not know what happened to most of the sick men that were left at various places along the march.

Q. What medical supplies were issued to you by the Germans on the march from Stalag Luft #4?

A. Very few. When we left the camp we carried with us a small amount of medical supplies furnished us by the Red Cross. At times the Germans gave us a pittance of drugs. They claimed they had none to spare. At various times, I asked for rations of salt. Salt is essential for the maintenance of body strength and of body fluids and minerals. This was particularly needed by our men because hundreds of them had lost tremendous amounts of body fluids and minerals as a result of dysentery. The only ration of salt that I have a record of or can recall was one small bag of salt weighing less than a pound. This was for about 2,500 men. I feel there is no excuse for this inadequate ration of salt.

Q. What were the circumstances which led to the deaths of [some of the] men?

A. About 8 March, 1945, while on the march in Germany under the jurisdiction of Stalag Luft #4, I set up a resting place for the sick at a barn in Beckendorf. Harold W. Mack was carried into this barn suffering from dysentery, malnutrition, exhaustion, frostbite, and impending gangrene on both feet. Permission to send him to a hospital was denied by Captain Weinert.

On March 9th our column was ordered to march about 6 kilometers. Sgt. Mack, and many others, was too weak to march so he was placed on a wagon and taken along. He was so weak at the time that he had to be spoon fed and carried to the latrine. On March 10th, after another appeal to Capt. Weinert, Sgt. Mack was sent back to Beckendorf to await shipment to a German hospital. Sgt. Mack had both feet amputated. According to the records of the Adjutant General, Sgt. Mack died in Germany on 2 April, 1945.

On February 24, 1945, I was operating a barn hospital at Bradenfeld, Germany, under the jurisdiction of Stalag Luft #4 on the march. Sgt. Trapnell was a patient at this hospital suffering from dysentery and exhaustion. In addition he developed symptoms of acute appendicitis which required surgery. Capt. Weinert authorized me to transport this patient by wagon to what he called a hospital at a nearby village of Bryge (or Brige). He must have known that a village of only a few people would not have a hospital. When I arrived at Bryge, I found that the so-called hospital was a barn with no medical facilities. Capt. Hay of the Royal Medical Corps was in charge of the sick there. He agreed with me that Sgt. Trapnell was seriously ill and that his acute appendicitis warranted immediate surgery.

We had no anesthetics or other supplies, not even a knife. We were both covered with filth. Capt. Hay hoped that he would be allowed to send Sgt. Trapnell to a German hospital the next day. I do not know how long it took to send St. Trapnell to a hospital for I had to rejoin my column at once. The records of the Adjutant General state that Sgt. Trapnell died 5 March, 1945.

Q. What other mistreatment did you suffer on the march from Stalag Luft #4?

A. There were beatings by the guards at times but it was a minor problem. At 1500 hours on 28 March, 1945, a large number of our men were loaded on freight cars at Ebbsdorf, Germany. We were forced in at the rate of 60 men or more to a car. This was so crowded that there was not enough room for all men to sit at the same time. We remained in these jammed boxcars until 0300 hours March 30, 1945, when our train left Ebbsdorf. During this 33-hour period few men were allowed out of the cars, for the cars were sealed shut most of the time. The suffering this caused was unnecessary for there was a pump with a good supply of water in the railroad yards a short distance from the train. At one time I was allowed to fetch some water for a few of our men who were suffering from dysentery. Many men had dysentery at the time and the hardship of being confined to the freight cars was aggravated by the filth and stench resulting from men who had to urinate and defecate inside the cars. We did not get off these freight cars until we reached Fallinbostel around noon on 30 March, 1945, and then we marched to Stalag 2B. The freight cars we were transported in had no markings on them to indicate that they were occupied by helpless prisoners of war. There was considerable aerial activity in the area at the time and there was a good chance of being strafed.

Q. Was the suffering that resulted from the evacuation march from Stalag #4 avoidable?

A. Certainly a large part of the suffering was avoidable. As I mentioned before, we marched through rural Germany and there was no lack of food there. There were always many large barns available that could have been used by us. There was always firewood available that could have been used to boil water and thus give us a supply of safe drinking water. There were many horses and wagons available that could have been used to transport our sick men. There were many men in our column who were exhausted and who could have been left for a rest at prison camps that we passed on the march.

On 30 March, 1945, we left the jurisdiction of Stalag Luft #4 when we arrived at Stalag Luft 2B. On 6 March (?) 1945 we again went on a forced march under the jurisdiction of Stalag 2B. Our first march had been in a general westerly direction, for the Germans were then running from the Russians. The second march was in a general easterly direction, for the Germans were then running from the American and British forces. Because of this, during the march under the jurisdiction of Stalag 2B, we doubled back and covered a good bit of the same territory we had just come over a month before. We doubled back for over 200 kilometers and it took 26 days before British forces liberated us.

Q. Are there any other incidents that should be reported?

A. There is one other incident I would like to report. On 16 February, 1945, we were on the road west of the Oder River in the general area of Schweinemunde. I was then marching with a party of several hundred of our stragglers who were tagging along behind our main column. We met a small group of other prisoners on the road. I was allowed to talk to these men briefly and obtained the following information: these men were from PW Camp Stalag 2B which had originally been at Hammerstein. They were all sick and had left their column to be taken to a hospital. On arrival at the hospital they were denied admission and continued to march with little or no rations. These men appeared to be on the verge of exhaustion. Two had obvious fevers with severe cough which was probably pneumonia or tuberculosis. About 20 of these men were Americans. One had on a foreign uniform and I thought he was an Italian. There was a tall British sergeant with them. One of the men carried a small wooden chest with the name of "Joe Mc-Daniels" or "Joe Williams" on it. He told me he had been acting Chaplain at Stalag 2B. Another man was a tall, slender fellow from Schenectady, New York. (After I was liberated I met an ex-prisoner from Stalag 2B who thought this fellow was J. Luckhurst of 864 Stanley, Schenectady, New York.)

This fellow said he was suffering from recurrent malaria. These men were so weak they could scarcely stand. The German sergeant in charge of our small section at the time recognized their plight and got a Wehrmacht truck to take them to our next stop. We received no rations that night but did get a small issue of hot water. The next day these men were placed on wagons and stayed with us. They again received no rations and again were sheltered in crowded barns. On 18 February, 1945, I personally protested to Capt. Weinert about these men, although he had known about them previously. I pointed out that these men were exhausted and might soon die. I requested rations, rest, and hospitalization for them. Capt. Weinert replied that no hospital was available. He further stated that these men were not his responsibility, inasmuch as they were not originally from Stalag Luft #4. I objected to this and stated that these men were now in our column and that he was responsible for their lives and health. He then agreed to leave these men behind. The next day, Capt. Weinert told me these men had been transferred to another command. I never saw the men again, but I heard a rumor that one of them had died.

After the war, Dr. Caplan went on to become a psychiatrist with an expertise in the issues of ex-POWs. While working at the Minneapolis Veterans Administration, he published numerous papers on their plight, and advocated for a standard disability compensation for all ex-POWs. He died in 1969 at the age of 61.

HAROLD KURVERS

From a letter to the President of the United States. Harold Kurvers resides in St. Paul, Minnesota.

Dear Mr. President:

On April 14, 1941, I was drafted into the army and sent to the Philippine Islands. From December 8th until the fall of Bataan we were under daily harassment by bombing or artillery fire and sometimes both. During this time we were on two meals a day, if we were lucky, and from January until April the two meals consisted of rice, soup, and whatever we could scrounge.

While on Bataan I came down with dysentery on numerous occasions and had malaria and dengue fevers. The diet and ailments caused me to lose about 20 pounds. I was on the Death March for seven, eight, or nine days, God only knows. I reached Camp O'Donnell weighing less than 100 pounds, and spent three months there under the most horrendous conditions. Our diet consisted of rice, weed soup, and water, and very little of each. The death rate was 50 to 60 men a day, and some days as high as 80.

In July, 1942, I was sent to Cabanatuan, a camp with conditions no better and the death rate about the same for the first three months. I remained there until September, 1944. While in this camp I had beriberi, pellegra, scurvy, yellow jaundice, dysentery, and numerous attacks of malaria and dengue fevers.

In September, 1944, I was moved to Bilibid Prison and was there until December 13 of the same year. On that date, 1,619 of us were taken to Manila Bay and crammed into the holds of a Japanese cargo ship where conditions were unbelievable. The very first night men went berserk, cutting throats and sucking blood, cutting their wrists to attempt suicide or for blood to quench their thirst, men screaming for water, some screaming for help and some drinking the urine they could emit. American planes bombed us the day after we boarded the ship, again on the second day, and finally sank us on the third day. The second ship we boarded was hit and so badly damaged we could go no further than Formosa. We boarded the third ship and were sunk before we could get underway. We reached Japan on the fourth ship 49 days after leaving Manila, having lost about 1,200 men and we who survived not weighing more than 80 or 90 pounds.

I was sent to a coal mining camp (Camp 17, Omuta) and after two months, weighing less than 100 pounds, went to work in the mine. I had to work 12 hours a day and 10 days in a row before a day off. While in Japan I contracted tuberculosis in both lungs. After liberation, September, 1945 until December, 1946, I was hospitalized in various hospitals. In July, 1958, I was hospitalized for eight months because of a tubercular kidney. From prison camp days to this very day I have had the aches and pains of an old man in my legs, left side, lower back, shoulders, and neck area. All these years I have had a very nervous stomach and very few days go by that I'm not as tense as a long-tailed cat in a room full of rockers.

Now the reason for this thumbnail sketch. I want to retire and apply for a 100% disability. I'm sure this is going to take a Presidential Order to accomplish this feat. In 1977, the Service Officer for the Veterans of Foreign Wars thought I should be compensated for my nervous condition. The Veterans Administration had other thoughts, claiming my problems were not service-connected. The decision was appealed, the Veterans Administration relented and awarded me 30% for anxiety but declared zero percent for my tuberculosis, an award of $66 I had been awarded in 1946. Would or could you sit still with this decision?

Finally, I don't think any captured defender of Bataan or Corregidor, after suffering nearly four years of hell, hunger, and indignities, should have to grovel for a compensation we have earned and deserve. Had you spent one day, any one day, of these years with us, I am positive you would be in total agreement.

JOHN W. WHIPPLE

From letter to the VA requesting a new compensation rating exam. Mr. Whipple is a resident of Tacoma, Washington.

It has taken me more than six months to set down a part of the history of my POW experience – not because I cannot remember the details, I remember them all too well, but because it causes me so much emotional pain that I am unable to describe more than one incident at a time, and sometimes only a small part of the incident. Whenever I try, it seems that I must relive the horror of those days emotionally, and often it is more than I can stand. I tend to joke about the things that happened, because if I didn't, I would either cry or scream.

A brief summary of my problems (since liberation) follows:

a. I have aches and pains in my shoulders, both arms, wrists and fingers, lower back, hips, both knees, ankles, and feet. The pain varies in intensity from day to day (and times of the day) but it is usually more intense in my right elbow, shoulder, and fingers. My arms and hands feel like they have gone to sleep often. I seem to lose all feeling in them; my upper arms feel somewhat different than do my hands. Sometimes I can't tell the difference between hot and cold water on them, although I sure can when cold water hits the rest of my body. It is very disturbing to feel that you are losing feeling in and/or control of one's hands and arms without any reason. I believe these problems originated in the Japanese prison camps because of the brutal beatings I was subjected to, and the severe cold and dampness I was forced to work and live in, and because of the extremely poor diet lacking in most necessary nutrients, including a complete lack of calcium.

b. I have episodes of upset stomach, cramps, and diarrhea about three times a month. This condition was caused by the lack of food, coupled with the stress of trying to stay alive. I am not contesting the Board's Rating of this impairment at this time. I'm listing it to show a total picture.

c. I have a large number of pre-cancer skin growths, caused by too much exposure to the sun. My lack of clothing as a POW left me exposed to the elements most of the time I remained in captivity.

d. My loss of hearing in my right ear is partially compensated with two hearing aids; however they are only effective when trying to hear a single speaker. Whenever I am in a room with many conversations, TV, or other noise, they are not effective at all. I believe that much of this hearing loss results from the beatings around the head which I suffered on almost a daily basis and the noise of four incendiary bombs which exploded within a radius of 10 feet of me in Osaka in April, 1945.

e. My wife of some 34 years divorced me in August, 1982. She was extremely angry and bitter, accusing me of all sorts of things I felt were untrue and unfair. She said I was angry all the time, I was cold and insensitive, uncommunicative, rigid, refused to admit I was ever wrong, always making very detailed plans before doing anything – never doing anything just for the heck of it, being too serious about everything (but at the same time she complained that I made a joke out of everything), that I was a perfectionist and expected everyone else to be perfect. She complained that I was always saving things; that I grew very upset about wasting anything, that I was very stingy with money (although she had a good house, appliances, food, clothing, etc.).

I was certain that she was just exaggerating her descriptions of me, and that what I felt and did and said were reasonable. She characterized me as being an exceptionally angry man, and always pessimistic and who would never change. I felt that she was saying that I was unique in my faults (compared to everyone else) and I felt that she was just being stubborn in refusing to see things my way at all, and finally feeling guilty because I wouldn't or couldn't change. It wasn't until I began meeting with other ex-POWs that I discovered that there was a great deal of truth in her perceptions of me, but that I was not unique in my feelings; most of the other POWs shared them.

f. In reflecting back on my work years, I can now see that many of the things which prevented me from rising higher in my field, and perhaps precipitated my early retirement were the unrecognized anger, distrust of others, my inability to relax and enjoy life, and my striving for perfection and demanding that perfection in others – perfection that I never seemed to attain.

g. I find it more and more difficult to cope with people. I can't get close to anyone – or let anyone get close to me. I do not trust anyone; I feel that everyone has a hidden motive, and I'm liable to come out on the short end of the stick if I deal with them. I feel emotionally flat – but that I must be on guard continually to make sure my emotions don't get out of hand. Although I get very angry, and I shout, etc., I remain in tight control of myself to prevent any kind of physical action knowing that if I released control, I could very easily kill a person.

*   *   *

I was a Marine attached to the American Embassy in Peking, China, when the Japanese bombed Pearl Harbor and Japan declared war against the USA. There were about 140 Marines in Peking, 42 in

Tientsin, and 23 in C'hin Wang Tao; 205 North China Marines. We had been ordered to leave North China on the SS President Harrison on December 10, presumably to return to the United States; as a result, most of our personal gear, arms, and ammunition had been shipped to C'hin Wang Tao. When the Japanese demanded our surrender, each Marine had his rifle (1903 Springfield), some NCOs and officers had a Colt .45 automatic pistol, and there was one case of .30 caliber ammunition in the compound. The Japanese had in excess of 100,000 troops in and around Peking (North China had been occupied by the Japanese since 1937). They had surrounded the compound with 75 mm guns, tanks, troops, and they had air support.

Colonel W.W. Ashurst, Commanding Officer, surrendered to the Japanese without firing a shot. He then ordered everyone under his command not to make any attempt to escape. He believed that we were to be considered to have diplomatic status under the conditions of the Boxer Protocol and a law passed in 1940, declaring that Marines stationed at a US Embassy as guards were considered to be diplomatic personnel.

At our surrender in Peking, the Japanese acknowledged that we were Embassy guards and said that we were not prisoners of war, but would be interned and treated like prisoners of war until we were repatriated. We remained confined to our barracks in Peking until my 21st birthday, January 10, 1942, when we were moved by train to the Marine barracks in Tientsin. What a way to celebrate reaching legal age. We remained in Tientsin until January 26, 1942.

On January 26, 1942 we were ordered to march to the railroad yards and loaded into very small boxcars (about 40 to a car). There wasn't enough room for everyone to lay or sit down. It was very cold – somewhere below zero not counting the windchill factor. There was no heat in the cars, only small open windows with bars across them near the top of the cars. The train started to move and we found there wasn't enough room to exercise to keep warm, so we just huddled together. Probably packing so many men in such a small space concentrated our body heat and prevented us from freezing to death.

The train would move and stop, move and stop, for a day and a half before the doors to the boxcars were opened. We had stopped at some small Chinese village, and were told to get out and marched into the center of the town (about a quarter of a mile away) to listen to a local official yell at us through a loudspeaker in Chinese or Japanese, I'm not sure which. It didn't make much difference because I didn't understand a word of his tirade. After he stopped yelling, we were marched back to the train and issued a small can (about 2 1/2 ounces) containing about four or five slices of some tasteless yellow vegetables packed in water. These cans were issued without any kind of opener, so we used whatever we could to get them open. This was the first food or liquid we had in two days.

*   *   *

We were assigned to old army barracks. The living quarters consisted of bays about 20x20 feet. Two raised platforms 8x20 feet faced each other; each platform contained nine cotton mattress bags filled with straw, and two light cotton blankets. The outside walls were made of 1x8 inch wooden planks, butted end to end and side to side (not lapped). They often had uncovered knot holes and broken spots so that the wind and rain or snow blew through them. There was no heat or facility to heat the building. It was cold – a cold that went clear through you, a cold that lasted for months, a cold that kept you from sleeping at night, that hurt almost as much as the hunger, and lasted and lasted until you couldn't think of anything else.

The next morning we were marched out in the rain and lined up to hear an address by Col. Yusi, Camp Commander. He told us all that we were cowards for surrendering, that our country didn't want us, our families and friends didn't want us and were ashamed of us; that the only honorable thing we cold do was to commit Hari-Kari. He even offered to provide the white cloth, sword, and instructions so we could do the job right.

This same message was repeated over and over again throughout the following weeks, and I mention it because we learned later that the U.S. State Department really made little or no effort to get the North China Marines repatriated as diplomatic staff. The Japanese knew by then that the United States did not insist that we be returned, and that we would not be repatriated. In addition, very few of us received any mail over the next few years, although some individuals did get lots of mail, and someone got mail every week or so to prove that mail was getting through, but nobody thought it worthwhile to write to most of us. It had a very demoralizing effect on most of us then; most were hurt, almost all were angry. And it still has an effect on me now, even though I realize letters were written but held up by the Japanese.

We received rice morning and night at first, and the soup at noon. Tea was supplied morning and night. Sometimes in the summer, the rice was exchanged for a small loaf of bread shaped like a large hamburger bun. While we were healthy, we spent our days waiting. Waiting for the Japanese roll call, breakfast, lunch, dinner, roll call, intermittent inspections/shake downs, beatings, rumors, news, wash clothing, fall out for a speech by the camp commander, wait, wait, wait. At night we would dream of food, of a warm, comfortable bed, of food, of getting out of the terrible, painful cold, of food. And we really had no idea how well off we were compared to what was to come.

* * *

We had two interpreters that I remember with great clarity. One was Isamu Ishihara, a former Honolulu cab driver who was one of the most brutal guards I have ever met. It was his daily practice to go through the barracks and beat prisoners with a club or 2x4. When a Japanese entered the barracks, we were required to stand at attention and bow when he passed. If one of us did not rise quickly enough or bow deeply enough or appear to be listening closely enough to suit Ishi, that person would be beaten about the head and upper body, often until he became unconscious. Very minor infractions, real or imagined, usually resulted in a severe face slapping, often knocking the person off balance.

There were prisoners, mostly in the Wake Islanders, who regularly acted as stool pigeons to the Japs for extra food, cigarettes, or an easier time. They had no reluctance to betray a fellow prisoner. For a long time we didn't know who they were, and there may have been some I still don't know about. It created a real atmosphere of distrust. You didn't dare get too close to anyone because he might turn you in to the Japs. I still find it very difficult to get close to others.

Towards the middle of April we were all aware of the fact that a ship (the *Gripsholm*) would be leaving Shanghai carrying repatriated United States citizens to Lourenco Marques and then to the United States. Many of us were sure that we would be repatriated on it and we gave much of our clothing, etc. to the Wake Island Marines. The *Gripsholm* left Shanghai about the 2nd of June, 1942, without us. While the disappointment was very great, we were assured that there was another ship, the *Conte Verde*, leaving in about two weeks and we would be on that. When the *Conte Verde* also left without us, we were told there was no room in it, so we were left. It was about this time we began believing what the Japanese authorities had been telling us since January – we were prisoners of war and we would not be going home until after the war was ended. This further deepened our feelings of loneliness, our distrust of others, our frustration, and feelings of abandonment – and served to further lower our morale.

* * *

With the warm weather came flies and mosquitoes, dysentery, and malaria. We were issued mosquito netting for each bay (nine men), but between the holes in the netting and the holes in the walls, it was not very effective. The Japanese offered to give us one cigarette for every five flies we caught and turned in. Some of the more enterprising men set up traps in the toilets and stayed in their vicinity all day collecting cigarettes. The cigarette deal only lasted one day before the Japanese issued an order that every prisoner must turn in five flies or they would not be fed. It reached the point where flies were bought and sold in order for some individuals to make their quota.

Many of us had diarrhea which would wax and wane throughout the year. I can remember one time I had severe diarrhea for 45 days, going to the toilet every 20 to 30 minutes, day and night, often passing nothing but a few drops of blood. I can still remember the day when I only made 13 runs to the toilet all day; I felt that I was over the worst and on my way to being cured. The diarrhea was accompanied by very severe cramps, with the pain so great that occasionally I passed out. One of the side effects of the diarrhea was the fact we got no rest or sleep. With no nourishing food and no rest, I became weaker and weaker. The medicine we were supplied for our illness was one (or both if the condition was very critical) of the two standard medicines the Japanese issued for the cure and/or prevention of all diseases: activated charcoal and brewers yeast. I suppose I'll never really know how effective these cure-alls were because my conditions seemed to me to be unchanged whether I took the medicine or not.

The weather grew colder and wetter. The mosquitoes and most of the flies died off, but the malaria attacks continued as did the diarrhea. The cold nights became more and more a problem. Between the pain of the cold, the having to get up and run to the toilets, and the guards' inspections, it was difficult – almost impossible – to sleep. We were weaker than we had all been led to believe.

About the middle of December we were all told we were going to be transferred to a new camp. We had to carry all the possessions we still had and fall in by barracks and bays to march about 15 miles to a new camp in Kiangwan. Shortly after our arrival (actually it was Christmas Eve) we were all issued a Red Cross Package (containing a pound of powdered milk, oleo, jam/jelly, 12-ounce can of corned beef, pack of cigarettes, and a chocolate bar). On Christmas Day, a retired soldier/ Shanghai restaurateur sent in a dinner for everyone. He had somehow secured permission from the Camp Commander to send in the dinner (the Japanese authorities and guards enjoyed it, too), gathered up 130 turkeys, borrowed ovens from other restaurants and bakeries and roasted them during the preceding week, and sent in turkey, dressing, potatoes for all 2,000 prisoners. The food really raised our morale.

* * *

In August, 1943, about 200 of us were chosen to be moved from Kiangwan. I really do not know on what the Japanese based their choices, because we were certainly a diverse group in experience, knowledge, physical condition, and military vs. civilian.We were just ordered to fall out of the lineup, gather up what personal things we had, march to some old canvas-covered army trucks, and taken to the docks in Shanghai. We were then loaded in the cargo hold of an old rusty Japanese freighter. We had nothing to lay on, and after they closed the hatch, we had no light. Most of us had the two cotton blankets we had been issued in Woo Sung, and we wrapped ourselves in them and waited. Finally the ship began to move, but none of us had any idea of where we were going – or why.

After 10 days, we arrived in what I later learned was Osaka, and marched about two miles to what was to be our home for the next 20 months, but at the time we didn't know that either. This camp was much smaller than either Woo Sung or Kiangwan. It consisted of five barracks, each of which held about 160 men. They were much smaller buildings, each bay holding 10 men on each side. There was also a much smaller barracks building at the far end of the camp that was used for a hospital. In addition, there was a coal shed, a small Japanese office, and a small building where the guards were quartered. The whole camp was surrounded by a tall wooden fence, topped with barbed wire. On the other side of the fence next to the building where I lived was a Japanese crematorium, and the smell of roasting/burning flesh was present most of the time.

The day following our arrival, we were marched about one and a half miles to the Fuji Nigata Ship Yards and divided up into work parties. My job, and that of most of our group, was stevedoring – loading and unloading ships and barges, carrying pipes, parts, supplies, and other heavy materials from one location to another. Our daily routine was to get up, make our beds and clean up the area, eat whatever food was available, line up and march to the shipyard to be at work by eight. We would work all day, and return to the camp about five. If we weren't too tired or sick we would wash clothes, repair our clothes or shoes, and wait for something to eat. After dinner, we would generally go to bed and try to get some rest.

One day while at work, we found a shed that had a barrel of dried, rolled bran that was used for feeding a horse used for heavy work. Several of us filled our pockets, clothes, or whatever we could find with this bran. We all tasted a little – ate a small amount – but one member of our crew sat down and ate a large amount. He munched on it while we worked, when he found an excuse to go to the benjo (toilet), and any other time he could. By afternoon he was extremely thirsty, and of course, he drank everything in sight. When all the liquid hit his stomach filled with dry bran, it expanded, and he began to suffer great pain (far greater than the usual dysentery cramps), and could not work. We became concerned about whether or not he would live, so we told our honcho he was sick and would have to go back to the camp. The guard said he could rest, but could not go back to camp until we all did. He grew worse during the afternoon, and finally the Japanese wanted to know what caused the trouble. After intense questioning, we told them that he had eaten the bran and drunk water.

At quitting time we were permitted to carry him back to the camp hospital where a Dutch doctor operated on him and removed much of the swollen bran, and he did survive. The Japanese called us crazy for eating the bran, and upon returning to the camp we were searched and they found some of the bran we had taken. The guards then made us stand at attention while they beat us with clubs for stealing the poor, hard-working horse's food. Then we had to stand at attention with arms outstretched holding a bucket full of water in each hand for four hours. Every time the arms would drop, the Jap guards would beat on us. That, they said, was very mild punishment.

*　*　*

During the two years I was in Japan, I received punishment for many real or imagined violations of regulations or codes. Usually they consisted of beatings about the head and upper body, but on two occasions the punishment was more severe. Once I had not properly bowed to a new civilian guard, and I was ordered to stand at attention with arms outstretched for hours. Every time my arms dropped, I was beaten. The sentence was reduced from 24 to eight hours because I told the military guard that I didn't think the civilian guard deserved as much respect as a soldier who had actually seen fighting.

The other time was in the winter of 1944 when one of the Wake Island Marines deliberately broke open a barrel of pickled daikons and was stealing some. I sneaked out of the shop, and got one, too. We were caught (I still believe one of the Marines who was playing footsie with the Japs tipped them off) and the guards questioned us as to who broke open the barrel. Neither of us would admit knowing so the guards made us kneel in front of their guardhouse in the freezing cold and placed a two-inch bamboo pole behind our knees, filled two buckets three-fourths full of water, and made us hold one in each hand, arms outstretched. They poured cold water over us, and every time we would drop an arm, we would be beaten, and more cold water poured on us. In this fashion they continued to question us. I lasted about three hours before I passed out. Finally, as I understand it, the other Marine confessed and he was kept in that position for 12 hours. I developed a new case of pneumonia, and he died later in the winter. Survival was not without stress.

That fall, one of my close friends, a North China Marine from Texas named Rodriguez, caught TB. He became weaker and weaker, and finally the Japanese admitted he could no longer work, and permitted him to stay in camp. Of course his rations were cut, but we made them up out of ours. Finally Rod decided that life wasn't worth the struggle, and decided to die. I can remember the last few days – he wouldn't eat, so I would feed him. I tried to talk with him about what we would do after the war (as we had so many times) but he wasn't interested. I tried insulting him, to get him angry enough to fight, but he was indifferent. No matter what I tried, it wasn't enough. He died in spite of my best efforts. I was angry – angry at myself because I couldn't help him, angry at him for dying and making me feel guilty, and angry at the Japanese for their treatment and lack of medical care. And I was sad, too. I still feel the same.

* * *

I made friends with a Japanese engineer who was educated in Germany. He could not speak any English, but between my poor Japanese and equally poor German, we did manage to communicate. He told me that all the Japanese were ordered to kill all prisoners if Japan was invaded; and that all men were to fight to the death and the women were to kill all the children and then commit suicide. When I asked him what he intended to do, he said that he did not know, but the honorable thing to do was what he had been told to do. He said that there was no doubt that all prisoners would be killed by someone. He told me that the United States planned to bomb Nigata (about 30 miles north of us) the next night, and it did fire-bomb that city. We could see flames all across the horizon. The next day he told me that the United States would bomb us the following night, and that the bombing had wiped out Hiroshima.

The following day we did not go out to work; the guards said that it was a holiday. The following night we went to work as usual and the next day he told me that Nagasaki had been bombed. Later in the day I heard a radio broadcast of Emperor Hirohito urging all Japanese to lay down their arms and surrender. He spoke of the terrible death and destruction in Hiroshima and Nagasaki. Many of the Japanese were crying.

We were soon returned to the camp and there was no work for several days. We didn't know whether the Japanese civilians and / or soldiers would try to kill us. The guards would tell us nothing; but my friend came by on the street and told me (over the wall) that we would be soon going home. It didn't quite work out like that, but at least some of us did get back.

* * *

In summary, the ailments I suffer from now are *all*, at least in part, directly connected to and stem from my experiences as a prisoner of war of the Japanese.

And the stress I feel now – perhaps more insidious because I have denied it in the past and feel almost ashamed to admit it now (a *man* should not let a little thing like that affect him) – causes me a great deal of emotional pain. I am filled with guilt, self-doubts, distrust, anger, frustration, fear, loneliness, and powerlessness. I have been subjected to such great stress as a POW to just stay alive, and such degradation and abuse by the enemy and by unthinking Americans after the war, and by such loneliness because I cannot establish deep, lasting relationships with other people or allow myself to feel any deep emotion (either joy or sorrow) because of my experiences as a POW, and I feel guilty because I feel that way. I believe that these feelings – these stresses – will be with me until I die. They have not diminished over the past 40-plus years, in fact, they seem to have intensified. And I believe *all* of these conditions are service-connected.

Regarding allegations of treasonous behavior by Wake Island prisoners of war: Mr. Whipple's observations concerning some of the Wake Island prisoners are solely his own. However, it should be acknowledged that conditions in the camps were so terrible that some men were driven mad. Further, it is known that the prison guards often attempted to induce a feeling of mistrust among prisoners. Whether the conduct described actually occurred or was instead the product of camp paranoia is a judgement I leave to others. I can bear no malice toward anyone who may have succumbed to temptation under such perilous circumstances.

Guy Kelnhofer, Jr.

THE ORYOKU MARU

The case of the Oryoku Maru presents one of the most heinous, shocking examples of cruelty by Japanese captors to Allied prisoners of war. A significant portion of the Tokyo War Crimes Trials were given to hearing testimony about the "hell ships." In the case of the Oryoku Maru, three-fourths of the 1,619 prisoners who boarded the ship had perished by the end of the journey. At the Trials, Mr. Alva C. Carpenter, Chief of the Legal Section, General Headquarters, Supreme Commander for the Allied Powers, had this to say: "Of all the cases of brutality and mistreatment accorded prisoners of war that have come out of World War II, none can compare with the torment and torture suffered by our soldiers . . . aboard the Oryoko Maru,* Brazil Maru and Enoura Maru . . . It is a saga of men driven to madness by sadistic and sensual captors . . . I have read diaries, written at the time, tomes of recorded testimony, have talked to survivors, and no place in recorded history can one find anything so gruesome and horrible. No mitigating circumstances can explain or condone such cruelty. The callous and vile conduct of the captors will live in infamy!"

The following excerpts are reprinted with permission from The Oryoku Maru Story, *a book prepared by Charles M. Brown in August 1983. Mr. Brown compiled this information from the official records of the Tokyo War Crimes Trials. He also prepared a list of the survivors of the three "hell ships," and their last known addresses, as of 1983. For further information about Mr. Brown's work, contact Tula Brown at 13680 Andover Drive, Magalia, California 95954.*

Summary of the Oryoku Maru story

The Oryoku Maru story actually involved three Japanese ships used to transport American and a few British prisoners of war from the Philippine Islands to Japan in the final months of the war (December 1944 - January 1945). The ships were the *Oryoku Maru, Enoura Maru* and *Brazil Maru.* It is important to note that the ships involved bore no markings to indicate that prisoners of war were crammed in the holds.

The prisoners of war were men who had been taken prisoner in Bataan, Corregidor and other locations in the Philippine Islands in April and May 1942. Some of them were survivors of the Bataan Death March, and all of them were survivors of approximately two and a half years in various Japanese prison camps where food and medicine were scarce, the work hard, and the death rate high.

After years had gone by without seeing any sign of American forces, the prisoners were elated when, in September, 1944, American airplanes

(*Both spellings of Oryoku have been used in the trials and since.)

flew over the camps and bombed Japanese military installations. This elation increased the following month, October, 1944, when news was received that American forces had landed on Leyte, less than 100 miles away. Everybody felt that liberation was finally close at hand.

This optimism was premature. The Japanese accelerated their efforts to transport prisoners of war to Japan during the last months of 1944 and early 1945. By this time, the seas and air were alive with American submarines and airplanes which were taking a heavy toll on Japanese ships. Unfortunately, many of these unmarked ships were carrying Allied prisoners in the holds. Some of them made it safely to Japan, others did not. Among those that did not make it were ships with prisoners of war aboard which were torpedoed by American submarines or bombed by American airplanes. Thousands of prisoners of war (American, British, Australian, and Dutch) lost their lives as a result of this activity.

In the case of the voyage of prisoners on the *Oryoku, Enoura* and *Brazil Marus*, it was American airplanes that did the damage.

During a lull in American air activity over Manila Bay in the latter part of November and early December, 1944, the Japanese were able to get some ships into the bay. On December 13, 1944, approximately 1,619 prisoners of war were marched from Bilibid Prison in Manila to Pier 7 (since renumbered 13) and loaded into three holds on the *Oryoku Maru*. Hold numbers one and three were very crowded, with number three being the worst of the two. Hold number two was the least crowded, with approximately 250 men assigned to it.

On the morning of December 14, 1944, the *Oryoku Maru* got underway in a convoy with other ships and naval escorts. The convoy passed Bataan and Corregidor and headed into the China Sea en route to Japan. American airplanes picked up the convoy almost immediately and bombed and strafed the ships all that day. Although the *Oryoku Maru* was damaged by the strafings and bomb "near misses," it managed to make its way into Subic Bay where it ran aground in the late afternoon. That evening the ship was towed to a location approximately 300 yards from the old U.S. Naval Station at Olongapo in Subic Bay. That evening the surviving Japanese passengers in the cabins were taken ashore; the prisoners of war were told that they would be taken ashore the next morning. The next morning (December 15, 1944), before the prisoners of war could be taken ashore, the American airplanes returned and bombed and strafed the ship. This time a bomb landed near the stern hatch of hold number three, killing many of the prisoners of war.

The survivors swam ashore, were recaptured by Japanese soldiers, transported by truck and train to Lingayen Gulf, placed on two ships (*Enoura* and *Brazil Marus*), and taken to Takao Harbor on Southern Formosa. All prisoners were consolidated on the *Enoura Maru*, which was bombed by American airplanes on January 9, 1945. The survivors were transferred to the *Brazil Maru*, which was not damaged in the bombing, and on January 13 departed for Japan. The *Brazil Maru* docked in Moji, Japan on January 31, 1945, with fewer than 500 living prisoners of war. Approximately 160 of these died shortly after arrival due to injuries or illnesses contracted during the voyage. While exact numbers are still not available, it is estimated that only 300 (18.5%) of the 1,619 prisoners survived the voyage.

Excerpts from Public Relations Information Summary Numbers 510 and 574, of the Tokyo War Crimes Trial (dated February 25 and May 9, 1947)

In [hold 3] the conditions were so crowded that the men, a few minutes after entering the hold, began fainting. The Japanese were asked to move some of the men out, the request was refused and they were told that there would be about 200 men put into the forward hold. There wasn't enough air and men were fainting due to the lack of air and intense heat. The Japanese were hurrying men into the hold, in some cases these men were being pushed down the stairs and beaten with rifle butts and shovels. Men were knocked down and off the ladder, falling on the men already below. In the lower bays they had to assume a crouched position because they couldn't stand upright. In the upper bays one could stand or crouch but could not lie down.

The [first] meal the prisoners received was the night of the 13th at 1900 hours. The meal amounted to nearly a full canteen cup of steamed rice and a teaspoon of salt and seaweed for each man, and one canteen cup of water for one whole bay of approximately 45 men. Each man received the equivalent of three teaspoons full of water. Other than this meager ration no food was received while the prisoners were aboard the *Oryoku Maru*, except on 14 December, men in the center hold received morning chow.

When the prisoners first boarded the ship there were a few cases of active diarrhea and dysentery. No provisions had been made for any latrine facilities in the holds. After repeated requests, four five-gallon buckets were lowered into the holds. They were placed in the corners. Although repeated requests were made to the Japanese for more buckets no action resulted. The four buckets that they received were overflowing within an hour and a half, and requests to empty them were refused. By 2400 hours the lower floor in the vicinity of the latrine was a sea of human waste. The stench in the hold was overpowering.

When the men first entered the ship, the temperature was between 85 and 90 degrees. About 0200 hours on the 14th, due to the noise and excitement, the hatch, which was the only opening for air, was completely battened down, cutting off all air except that which seeped through the hatch cover. The temperature then rose to about 120 degrees. Men against the bulkheads, in the bays, were passing out for lack of air. These men were removed to the front of the bay where they were revived.

During the nights of the 13th and 14th men became deranged and would wander about the hold stepping on other prisoners, screaming for water and air. Some became violent to the extent that they lashed out with canteens or striking with their fists or feet at anyone with whom they came in contact. It was pitch black in the hold. In this chaos there was no possibility for much-needed sleep. On this first night about 40 to 50 men went out of their minds.

At about 0800 hours [the morning of the 14th] an air raid alarm sounded. The ship was strafed, ricochets began flying into the holds. The ship had been damaged, and was moving now with difficulty. Several men had been wounded during the raid by the ricochets. During the air raid it was learned that at least 30 men had died in the aft hold the night of the 13th, mostly due to suffocation. After the raid, medical groups were called on deck to treat the Japanese wounded. When requests were made for medical aid for men in the holds, and food and water, they were beaten up and told that the Japanese would do nothing for prisoners.

On the night of the 14th, and the morning of the 15th, conditions grew worse. Men were suffering from thirst so acutely that many went out of their minds. Much screaming was audible. There was almost a complete lack of discipline, no matter how hard the hold leaders tried to restore order. The need for water was so acute that the men were drinking their own urine and sewage running in the open drains along the side of the ship. These hideous actions were revealed to the Japanese but there was no action taken. The hold was a bedlam with screaming, swearing, fighting. Men went berserk and the conditions were like some fantastic nightmare.

On the morning of the 15th the ship was anchored in Subic Bay. About 0930 hours, the order for the evacuation came through. Several of the guards fired into the holds prior to evacuation. Prior to this order there had been an air raid in which a direct hit on the aft hold had been made, and about 100 men were killed. There were no life preservers or lifeboats in evidence. Men were forced over the side of the ship with no regard given as to whether or not they could swim. During the swim for shore some of the men got aboard the debris from the ship and attempted to float ashore. In one case a raft with five men on it was fired upon by a machine gun set up on the shore. Two of the men on the raft leaped off into the water, the remaining three were killed.

Once on shore the prisoners were assembled into the area adjacent to a tennis court. During the period of assembling, the men were permitted to fill their canteens at a water tap outside the tennis court, but to do this they had to stand in line four to six hours. Fifty percent of the prisoners received their first water since the night of the 13th, the rest didn't get any because the Japanese, as a result of the confusion, chased them back into their assembly area.

At roll call there were fewer than 1,300 prisoners still alive out of the 1,619 that had left Manila. No food was issued on the 15th or the 16th, and the water situation was still very bad. On the evening of the 17th one sack of uncooked rice was issued for 1,300 men. This amounted to about two tablespoons full for each man. The same amount of rice was issued on the 18th and 19th. On the 20th the ration increased to four tablespoons full. All of this was eaten raw.

On the morning of 20 December, 1944, 500 of the men were taken to San Fernando, Pampanga, and the second group left on the 21st. The first group was placed in the provincial jail, and the second group in the movie house. While there, the prisoners were finally issued a canteen of rice. There was a spigot at the theater with running water and by keeping order, everybody received enough water. Ample water was also available at the jail.

About 1900 hours a truck was brought to where the group was waiting and [15 of] the sick were driven in the truck to a small cemetery on the outskirts of San Fernando, Pampanga. When they arrived at the cemetery there were a group of soldiers who had dug a hole about 15 feet square. When the guards on the truck had dismounted, they took up positions about the hole. Two of the guards brought one of the prisoners to the hole. He was told to kneel at the edge of the hole and to take a position as though in prayer. The prisoner was bayoneted and decapitated. This procedure was followed until all 15 of the prisoners had either been bayoneted or decapitated.

From San Fernando, Pampanga, the prisoners were moved by train to San Fernando, La Union, on 24 December. The prisoners were marched to the railroad station. Forty men who were the sickest were allowed to be placed on top of the cars. In the train, the conditions were very bad. The heat was terrific, and due to crowding and lack of air many men passed out. When a man became unconscious he was passed from hand to hand to the door of the boxcar to revive.

The train arrived at San Fernando, La Union, about 0500 hours Christmas morning of 25 December, 1944. The weather was bitterly cold. At nine a.m., orders were received that the men were to line up and prepare to march to the beach. After remaining on the beach for two days and two nights, on the morning of 27 December, the first group of 236 men were loaded aboard the *Brazil Maru*, the remainder of the men on the beach were loaded aboard the *Enoura Maru*. The men were marched to the piers where landing barges were waiting to carry the men out to the transports. While loading into the barges men were compelled to jump from the pier into the barges, some 20 feet below.

If a man hesitated before jumping to the barge the guard would push him off the pier. In several instances men broke their legs. In one case, one man missed the barge completely, hitting his head on the side of the barge and falling into the water. When this man was finally dragged into the barge, he was dead.

The *Brazil Maru* was an old freighter of about 2,500 tons. During the six-day trip from the Philippines to Takao, Formosa, no food was received during the first two days except the food leavings of the five Formosan guards. This amounted to about one teaspoon of rice per man. On the third day an issue was made which was three men per mess kit of food. On the fourth day there was no food at all. On the fifth day prisoners were issued five Japanese rolls per man. These rolls were a type of hard tack infested with maggots and mold.

All of the prisoners on the *Enoura Maru* (about 10,000 tons), were confined to one hold with two levels, forward of amid-ships. The condition was very crowded but not as bad as on the *Oryoku Maru*. A man could lie down here by doubling up his legs. 236 men were moved from the *Brazil Maru* to the *Enoura Maru* in Takao Harbor, on or about 6 January, 1945.

On 9 January in mid-morning, during the completion of the morning meal, anti-aircraft fire was heard on the *Enoura Maru* and all ships in the harbor. Soon the drone of planes was heard and almost simultaneously the whistle of bombs was heard. The *Enoura Maru* rocked violently from a near miss, causing a flail of bomb fragments and steel fragments from the sides of the ship which killed about 300 outright and injured a considerable number. After the bombing, such first aid as could be rendered to men was made available by the prisoner of war doctors and corpsmen aboard. This aid consisted of collecting dirty towels, undershirts, or anything that could be used for bandages that the other prisoners would contribute.

The dead bodies in the holds were stacked in the center of the hatch area like stacks of cord wood. They remained there until the 12th of January.

Finally in mid-morning of 12 January, permission was granted to remove the dead bodies from the ship. The scene in the holds was like a page from Dante's Inferno — dark, but one could see the wraithlike figures wandering dazedly through a maze of stacked corpses. It was not uncommon prior to the removal of the dead to sit on the dead and eat meals due to the overcrowded conditions. Items of salvageable clothing that could be removed from the dead were removed. Many of the bodies were in various stages of decomposition when they were finally removed.

On 13 January, during the afternoon, orders came through that all the prisoners aboard the *Enoura Maru* would be transferred to the *Brazil*

Maru. Reasons for this change were that the *Enoura Maru* had been badly damaged during the bombing. Transfer to the *Brazil Maru* was effected by landing barges. At this time, there were approximately 900 men remaining alive out of the original group of 1,619. The ship sailed from Takao on the 13th of January for Japan.

During the journey there was active trading for rings, watches, and fountain pens between the prisoners and the Japanese guards and the ship's crew for food, water, and cigarettes. A lot of West Point and other graduation rings were traded for a cup of water or 10 cigarettes. Anyone who had anything to trade did so.

The water situation was very acute for the first two days out of Takao harbor; no liquids of any kind were issued. On the 15th day, and approximately twice a day until the 29th, water was spooned out. It was black, salty and unpalatable. At no time, even when the death rate was at its highest, was the amount of water increased.

Medical facilities aboard the ship were nil. Only the more seriously sick were placed under the hatch which was considered as the hospital area. It was the coldest spot on the ship. Whenever a man was placed in sick bay it was almost a certainty that he would die. It is said that one large bottle of sulfathiazol pills aboard the *Brazil Maru* probably would have saved at least 100 men whose diarrhea was a contributing cause to their death.

The odyssey ended on or about 30 January, 1945, when about 450 half-naked emaciated corpses shivered down the gangplank of the *Brazil Maru* in Moji, Japan. Of those who disembarked in Moji, not one was able to walk normally and more than one-half [were] carried ashore. Many died within a few weeks as a result of the trip. Today [1947] it is estimated there are about 200 to 300 of the original 1,619 men who boarded the *Oryoku Maru* in Manila still alive.

APPENDIX 2
Questioning Japan's Honor

Does time heal all wounds? In the 50 years since the bombing of Pearl Harbor, no Japanese official has ever issued an apology to America, a slight still taken to heart by many Americans. In 1991, Japan's prime minister did apologize publicly to North and South Korea, to Canada, and to the countries of East Asia, but not to the Philippines or the United States.[1] Perhaps the closest thing to an apology to America were the remarks made by the mayor of Nagasaki in 1988 suggesting that Emperor Hirohito shared culpability for the war. Voicing those opinions was complete heresy to many Japanese; indeed, the mayor was later shot and wounded by a right-wing conservative who did not agree.[2] The truth seems to be that the Japanese are not ready to discuss their country's actions during the war. The question is, can they afford not to?

The issue of an apology is of prime importance to the survivors of Japan's prison camps. Japan's failure to acknowledge wartime brutality and apologize for it stands in the way of the survivor's healing process. We need to forgive our captors, but that is an impossible task if Japan will not acknowledge its crimes and ask our pardon. Without such an apology we are stuck in our recovery, burdened with an unbearable load of hate and rage.

There are certain events which change the world. Our world was never the same after December 7, 1941. That day began as a peaceful Sunday until the calm was shattered in Pearl Harbor, Hawaii. People on their way to church or just sitting down to breakfast found their ordered world destroyed suddenly by wave after wave of bombing and strafing Japanese war planes. This was how the Japanese government informed the United States that war was declared. It was truly a "day of infamy".

The long, bloody war that followed that unprovoked attack stands out as a watershed event in the history of Japan and the United States. Yet, it is a conflict which now is largely forgotten and seemingly ignored by the current generation of Americans and Japanese. Our lapse in memory is partly the result of deliberate policy. Through a judicious mix of revisionist history and censorship, Japan tries to escape reminders of her past mistakes. America also downplays this aspect of our relations with Japan as we seek to build strong ties to a country that has become an important economic and political ally.

This conspiracy of silence endangers the development of trust which both countries strive to achieve in their transactions with each other. Aftereffects of that war linger because of persistent questions that will not allow the conflict to settle. Japan and the United States need to move beyond these last doubts if we are to have a durable peace and ensure harmonious relations between our two peoples.

Lingering Suspicions

More than 40 years have passed since Japan was forced to give up its grandiose plans of establishing through military conquest a Greater East Asia Co-Prosperity Sphere.[3] When Japan surrendered in 1945, its economy was destroyed, its major urban centers were piles of smoldering rubble, and its people were starving. Despair and fear gripped the defeated Japanese. There was a widespread expectation that the victorious Americans would deal as harshly with the defeated civilians of Japan as Japan's own forces had dealt with the populations of the territories they had so recently occupied.

But Japan did survive, and prosper. Through the generosity of the American people, the humanity and vision of General MacArthur, and the industriousness of the Japanese workers, Japan rebuilt its economy. Today Japan is recognized by the world community for its wealth, its inventiveness and its productivity. The discipline of its labor force is admired and its production techniques are studied and emulated throughout the world.

Americans find it admirable that our former enemy has risen from the ashes of defeat to become a world-renowned economic success. Many of us, however, temper our admiration for Japan's progress with a gnawing suspicion about that country's ambition concerning economic and political leadership. We are not sure that Japan is really the trustworthy ally that it purports to be.

Looking back on Japan's past behavior, many Americans question whether the present economic contest between our two countries is wholly peaceful in its intent. Some have suggested that this economic rivalry constitutes a strategic continuation of the struggle that we thought was ended in the surrender ceremonies aboard the *USS Missouri* in 1945. It seems to many Americans that Japan gave up the military phase of its campaign of domination, but failed to give up its imperialist ambitions.

Are these unwarranted suspicions? Is there reason to believe that Japan is not an honorable nation in which we can safely place our trust? How well would the Japanese score on tests of ethical standards in foreign relations?

The Question of Honor

Foreign observers have commented on the high regard accorded to personal honor by the people of Japan. Affronts to a man's dignity, to his family name or to his community reputation are deadly serious matters to a Japanese. We Americans share many of these same values, respecting courage, honesty, and integrity. Unlike the Japanese, however, we seldom feel impelled to commit suicide to redeem our honor as a consequence of some social disgrace. The Japanese code of honor appears to be more demanding in that respect.[4]

And yet, reviewing Japan's international conduct in the past, we Americans find it difficult to understand how that conduct conforms to our own concepts of honorable behavior. We wonder whether the Japanese may have two different codes of honor: one for their interpersonal and community behavior and another for their behavior abroad. Perhaps the Japanese regard foreigners as little more than brute barbarians whose approval is not a worthy goal and who may safely be ignored.

For example, in 1941 Japan launched a surprise military attack against the United States while their diplomats were negotiating with ours in Washington, D.C. From an American point of view, that was a treacherous and cowardly action which an honorable people would not countenance. Yet, the men who were responsible for that unprincipled act, whose policies brought their country to the very brink of annihilation, are today honored and respected by the people of that country.[5] We wonder how to interpret these examples of Japan's concern for international honor.

Americans do not understand how an honorable people could give their allegiance to a military organization which won the reputation of being one of the most brutal and merciless in the annals of history. Testimony at the Tokyo Tribunals by witnesses, survivors, and participants proved beyond any doubt that Japanese troops regularly engaged in acts of murder, mutilation, rape, arson, infanticide, and cannibalism. Japanese military photographers even filmed such atrocities as the Rape of Nanking. There, in 1937, hundreds of thousands of innocent Chinese civilians were tortured and butchered in a bloody rampage that went on for 40 days.[6] Is this the behavior of an honorable people?

The many victims of Japanese cruelties during World War II find it especially difficult to forgive their enemies for their transgressions. The Japanese pretend that there is nothing to forgive. They admit to no wrongdoing. Americans believe that an honorable person admits his errors and tries to atone for any injuries he has caused to innocent parties through his neglect or misconduct.

Revising the Past vs. Making Reparation

Newspaper accounts of the past decade tell us about how Japanese leaders are trying to cover up Japan's misdeeds. Seizuki Okuno, director general of the national land agency, declared that Japan, the country that occupied Korea, invaded China, and attacked the United States in peacetime, was not an aggressor nation in World War II. His views, we read, were supported by 41 members of the governing Liberal Democratic Party.[7] In 1986, Education Minister Masayuki Fujio wrote in a magazine article that Korea was partly to blame for its occupation by Japan in 1910.[8] In 1989, the Education Ministry won a lawsuit allowing for the continued "screening" of school textbooks. Under the Ministry's control, the Rape of Nanking became simply "chaos" in which many civilians and soldiers were killed. Neither will Japanese students learn of the torturous medical experiments conducted on prisoners of war at the Imperial Army's Unit 731; that part of history has been deleted altogether for lack of academic documentation.[9] Other changes attempted by the Education Ministry have included describing the invasion of China as an "advance," and calling the forced transfer of Koreans to Japan an "implementation of the national mobilization order to the Koreans."[10]

In 1988, the press carried reports of the efforts of the Shochiku Fuji Co. to delete from the film "The Last Emperor" the scenes depicting Japanese atrocities in the occupation of Nanking.[11] These are examples of Japanese attempts to escape the consequences of their behavior by lies and evasions. Americans would condemn such a course of action as both cowardly and dishonorable. How do the Japanese justify this as the proper conduct of an honorable people?

Following World War II, the German government acknowledged its guilt and confessed its shame for the atrocities committed by the German people under the rule of the Nazi party. To show its repentance, German leaders have gone to Israel to lay wreaths at memorials dedicated to the victims of the Holocaust. Reparations have been paid by the German government to many of those who were the objects of the criminal acts of the German people in World War II. An honorable people could do no less.

Contrast this civilized behavior with that displayed by Japan, a country that professes to place great importance on upholding its national honor. No Japanese leader has come to Pearl Harbor to lay a wreath on the sunken *USS Arizona* and its entombed crew. To my knowledge, no Japanese leader has ever come forward to any American forum to admit that Japan engaged in atrocious behavior in its treatment of Allied prisoners of war; or declared that the Japanese people are truly sorry for the terrible suffering they caused by their actions in World War II.

Future Relations

It would be naive to believe that these few words here will move the Japanese to respond with appropriate expressions of remorse and a request for America's forgiveness. Convinced of their racial and cultural superiority, they see themselves as a chosen people, descendants of the sun god, with a destiny of leadership to fulfill.[12] Apparently, those inferior peoples who would stand in the way of that ordained mission must suffer the consequences. More than likely, the majority of the Japanese people have never felt and may never feel any shame about the atrocities committed by their troops in World War II. Our sense of what is proper behavior among nations seems to be foreign to Japanese cultural standards. This observation is made without implying any disrespect or supposing inferiority to the Japanese because of these differences from our own cultural norms.

Nevertheless, it is important for the Japanese to understand that they are regarded with suspicion in the West because of their failure to respect our Western sensibilities. Former enemies of Japan retain a deep and abiding mistrust of the Japanese.[13] How could it be otherwise? This distrust is not likely to abate so long as Japan continues to indicate to the world that it will judge its behavior by its own internal standards of national honor and will ignore outside opinions and foreign notions of rectitude.

Pragmatic considerations alone should convince the Japanese that the way foreigners view Japan can have important effects for the export-dependent economy of their country. There must be many hundreds of thousands of foreign customers who will not buy goods made in Japan regardless of its merits. They have long memories and they harbor resentment against the Japanese for the way they or their friends and relatives were treated by Japan during World War II. Some of these disaffected people are influential individuals in commerce, government, and finance. It would be in the best interests of Japan to cultivate the good opinion of these important people who do not feel comfortable dealing with the Japanese or buying Japanese products.

The time has come for Japan to recognize and satisfy America's legitimate aspirations for resolving this unsettled business which continues to divide us. Japan has many moral debts to settle in America if she is to satisfy her creditors and close her accounts on World War II. Although it might not prove feasible for Japan to compensate properly the remaining foreign survivors of the Japanese prison camps, much could still be done to alleviate the economic consequences visited on their widows and children.

Trust funds, scholarships, endowed university chairs, the establishment of specialized hospitals, and the funding of research institutes are just a few examples of the measures Japan might take to demonstrate its concern for the victims of its criminal behavior. Japanese commercial interests also have a role to play in this accounting. Japanese industrial conglomerates benefited economically during World War II by employing prisoners of war as slave laborers to unload their ships, mine their coal and pour their steel.[14] Back wages, plus interest, could be paid to survivors of the former prisoners of war who made up these slave labor parties.

Western sensibilities and public opinion would be affected in a very positive way if a respected Japanese leader were to deliver a personal apology for the unprovoked attack on the United States in 1941. A public act of contrition would redound to the benefit of Japan and go far to strengthen the relations between our two countries. Such an act of statesmanship would win worldwide attention and engender a significant shift of world opinion in favor of Japan.

It may be that Japan has abided by its own concepts of its national honor. But unless it takes steps along the lines suggested here, there is little prospect that Japan will be regarded as an honorable nation in the world that America represents.

Guy Kelnhofer, Jr.

APPENDIX 3
Medical Effects of Incarceration

No discussion of the former POW's life after liberation would be complete without a look at the medical effects of captivity. Below is a brief examination of the diseases commonly suffered by prisoners of war and the post-liberation symptoms. This is by no means an authoritative, nor an exhaustive treatment of the subject. Rather, the information presented is meant to serve as an introduction to the medical effects of captivity. All information was gathered from previously published articles and studies, which are listed. If you believe you or someone you know may be affected by these diseases, you are urged to contact your doctor or VA hospital immediately. Thanks to Brian Engdahl, Ph.D., and Raina E. Eberly, Ph.D., both of the Minneapolis VA Medical Center, and to Dr. William Shadish, a member of the National Advisory Committee on Former Prisoners of War, for their assistance in reviewing this chapter.

Some effects of starvation, or avitaminosis (vitamin deficiency)

Beriberi – resulting from lack of vitamin B_1 (thiamine). Defined in two categories: wet beriberi, which affects the heart, and dry beriberi, which affects the nervous system. Cardiac symptoms, which range from irregular heart rate to shortness of breath and swelling of the heart, can lead to death. Beriberi affecting the nervous system can result in pain, cramping or a burning sensation in the limbs, especially the legs and feet, and in motor disability. Severe cases may result in difficulty swallowing or hoarseness, loss of hearing and loss of vision; paralysis of the limbs is a rare but possible outcome. Some damage caused by beriberi is permanent; other symptoms can be relieved with replenishment of B vitamins. Approximately 77% of all ex-POWs from the Philippines were found to have a history of wet beriberi; 50% had suffered from dry beriberi. In instances where there has been prolonged and severe nutritional deprivation, as in an Asian POW camp, it is common to find both types of beriberi in the patient. (10)

Numbers refer to sources listed at the end of this appendix.

Loss of libido – according to one study, by Dr. E.C. Jacobs, loss of libido in the camps was a common result of malnutrition, particularly for the Pacific POWs. Other symptoms included loss of hair follicles and thinning and loosening of the skin, which might indicate a decrease in the production of the male sex hormone. Continued problems with impotence after repatriation might also be symptomatic of psychological distress, as with some ex-POWs who suffer from depression or from post traumatic stress disorder. (5, 10)

Nerve deafness – caused by degeneration of the Organ of Corti, in the inner ear, resulting in permanent high tone deafness. (13)

Neuritis – defined as inflammation of a nerve or its parts. A result of vitamin B deprivation, of some infections, or of compression of the nerve. Effects of neuritis might include loss of vision, loss of hearing, painful or numb hands and feet. Symptoms may take years to appear. (8)

Nutritional blindness — caused by a lack of vitamin A; can result in permanent damage to the central area of the retina, affecting night vision and ability to read small print. Sometimes results in blindness. (8, 10)

Pellagra – resulting from lack of niacin. Symptoms include dermatitis, diarrhea, and dementia. The dementia takes the form of insomnia, irritability, nervousness, anxiety, and depression. Symptoms are relieved when niacin is replaced; however, severe dementia may be untreatable. Severe atrophy can result, possibly leading to psychoses and, in some instances, to death. (9, 10)

Scurvy – resulting from lack of vitamin C. Affects the body's ability to heal wounds, maintain bone strength, and maintain blood vessels. Symptoms include bruises and hemorrhages, bleeding gums, joint pain, anemia. (10)

Weight loss – usually extreme. POWs liberated from camps in the Pacific and Korea lost an average of 40-50% of their pre-internment body weight. Better nutrition and a shorter length of imprisonment account for the lesser weight loss in German camps – about 30% of original body weight.Recent research has shown a correlation between the severe weight loss of former POWs and their illnesses later in life. (9, 10)

Diseases common in the POW camps

Amebic Dysentery (Amebiasis) – caused by the parasite Entamoeba Histolytica. Extremely common in the camps. Symptoms range from chronic mild diarrhea to ulcerations of the intestinal wall and extreme dysentery. Can result in abscesses in the liver, producing hepatitis symptoms; can also travel to the lungs. Although it is easily cured with drugs or through natural immunity, amebiasis has been known to linger for several years after onset. (2, 10)

Conjunctivitis – inflammation of the eyeball lining. It is often a symptom of a virus, parasites or bacteria, and can be extremely infectious, particularly in virus-caused cases. Serious cases can lead to blindness if untreated. (3, 9, 10)

Dengue Fever – caused by a virus transmitted by mosquitoes in tropical climes. Symptoms include muscle weakness, excruciating pain — especially behind the eyes and in joints, high fever, and sometimes skin rash. May take weeks for recovery and second episodes are not uncommon. (1, 10)

Fungal skin infections – especially common to malnourished POWs, fungal infections can occur above the skin, as in ringworm, or below the surface. A common form is athlete's foot. Other fungal infections may occur on the upper trunk, on the inner thighs, on the scalp, in the beard, or on the fingernails. Most are treatable with antifungal agents. (2, 10)

Giardiasis – caused by a parasite (giardia lamblia) in the gastrointestinal tract. Noted by diarrhea, gas, cramps, or nausea, which stop after treatment. However, as many as two-thirds with giardiasis experience no symptoms. Recurrence of symptoms is rare without reinfection. (3, 9)

Hepatitis – characterized by lethargy and weakness, an enlarged liver and sometimes jaundice or yellow skin pigmentation. Generally caused by a virus, which can be transmitted by flies and impure drinking water, or through the blood or urine of an infected person. Symptoms may be short-lived or lingering; permanent liver damage can result, and death may follow. (2, 10)

Hookworm (Ancyclostomiasis) – larvae are absorbed through the feet or ingested by mouth, and eventually deposit in the small intestine, where they can become quite large. As the worms burrow into the intestinal walls, the host can lose up to four ounces of blood a day, resulting in anemia and severe iron deficiency. Hookworms can live this way for several years. Diagnosis requires identification of the eggs in the stool; treatment with drugs is usually successful. (1, 10)

Malaria – caused by a parasite transmitted to the blood system by the bite of the female anopheles mosquito. Can be fatal. Symptoms may include enlarged or ruptured spleen, enlarged liver. Some believe malaria may lead to hepatitis, although this connection has not been conclusively proven. Enlarged kidneys, congested blood vessels and strokes may also result. Some types of malaria can recur in the system for years after the initial infection. (1, 9, 10)

Roundworm (Ascaris lumbricoides) – the eggs of the giant roundworm – which can grow to 15" in length – are transferred to the mouth through contact with fecal matter. They hatch and settle in the intestinal tract, where they reproduce. Symptoms of roundworms can include severe malnutrition and intestinal blockage as the parasites feed off the host body. Diagnosed through stool samples and treated with drugs. (10)

Scabies – skin infection caused by a mite, which is easily spread by contact with infected skin, clothing, or blankets. Leads to itching and burrow-shaped lesions on the skin which can become infected ulcers. Easily treated with ointments. (10)

Strongyloides (threadworms) – caused by an intestinal worm found in tropical climates. Considered one of the most chronic of illnesses suffered by former Pacific and Korean POWs, strongyloides has been found in patients more than 35 years after liberation. The worm larvae commonly enter the body through the mouth, or the skin of the feet, then invade the bloodstream and travel to the lungs and intestines. Symptoms can include scratching cough, bloody sputum, abdominal pain, cramps, diarrhea, and bloody stool. Since the worms reproduce themselves in the body, long-term infection is very possible. The best detection method is by intensive microscopic examination of the stool. Ordinary microscopic study will prove unreliable; it may take many tests to confirm the presence of the worm. (1, 10)

Tuberculosis – caused by a bacterium that attacks the lung tissue, which can erode into the blood vessels. Characterized by fatigue, night sweats, cyclical fevers, coughing up blood, loss of body weight. Sometimes spreads into other areas of the body. Considered a killer of World War II POWs for years after liberation, although most occurrences of tuberculosis are treatable today. Infected persons may carry the germs for a lifetime with no side-effects, or may experience the illness years after infection. (2, 10)

Ulcerative impetigo – skin infection resulting from bacteria. Ulcers can form on legs and arms, and can be deep and painful. Scarring is common. Easily treatable today with antibiotics. (3, 10)

Note: Sixty to seventy percent of all Pacific POWs, and 40% of Korean POWs had intestinal parasites at the time of repatriation. Many of the Pacific POWs harbored from two to six different species of parasites.(10)

Other common ailments

Gingivitis – the early stage of periodontal (gum) disease, caused by poor hygiene, vitamin deficiency and some glandular and blood disorders. Symptoms include swollen, bleeding gums and persistent bad breath. Also related to Trench Mouth, where inflamed areas of the gums are coated with a greyish-yellow membrane. Gingivitis, tooth decay (caries) and periodontitis all can lead to the loosening and eventual loss of teeth. POWs were especially prone to dental problems. In the Korean camps, gravel in the rice caused some broken teeth and lost fillings. In the German camps, it is reported that dentures were issued only after 15 or more teeth had been lost. And a study of repatriated

Canadian POWs after World War II showed that most suffered from gingivitis or pyorrhea, and had lost many or all of their teeth. (2, 11, 12)

Liver Damage – a study of 4,684 British POWs from World War II found that 803, or nearly 18%, had been treated for liver abnormalities within five years of liberation. The damage ranged from mild problems to cirrhosis and liver cancer. Most damage seemed to stem from three causes: viral hepatitis, intestinal parasites, and malaria, all originating in the prison camps. Damage was often exacerbated by high levels of alcohol use by repatriated POWs. By the mid-1970s, few of the study subjects still suffered from liver problems. Most were either cured, or had already died from the effects. Chronic liver damage may also be traceable to malnutrition. (10, 13)

Osteoarthritis – or degenerative arthritis, degenerative joint disease, osteoarthrosis. A common disease among the aging, considered by some to be highly prevalent in former POWs. Characterized by joint pain, swelling and stiffness, due to loss of cartilage and the erosion of joint surfaces. Former POWs may be more severely affected because of the combined effects of starvation and excessive physical labor during captivity. For most POWs, malnutrition depleted the body of muscle mass and cartilage, leaving the skeletal system with little protective tissue. Carrying heavy loads in this condition then taxed the joints and vertebrae, resulting in microtrauma and eventual erosion of the joints. (8, 10)

Post-Traumatic Osteoarthritis – pain or stiffness in particular bones or joints, likely caused by specific injuries, such as a blow from a rifle butt, or broken bones received in a beating. (7, 10)

Psychological effects

Depression – found to be more common in former POWs than in the general population. In a survey of former World War II and Korean War POWs, conducted from 1984-1989, between 37 and 57% were found to have symptoms of depression. The "normal" rate of depressive symptoms for mid-age males is 10%. The report also found that the probability of depressive symptoms rose in proportion to body weight lost in camp: the higher the weight loss, the higher the probability of depressive symptoms. (6)

KZ Syndrome – or concentration camp syndrome. First documented in the 1940s and 1950s in Europe, following the liberation of concentration camp survivors. Not commonly recognized or diagnosed by U.S. doctors, although Scandinavian countries have legislated entitlements for KZ Syndrome. Thought to be a direct result of famine and nutritional deficiency, resulting in impairment of the immune system and damage to the brain, myocardium and other tissue. Recognized symptoms, in order of frequency, include: increased fatigue; nervousness, irritability and restlessness; memory impairment; dysphoric mood; emotional instability; sleep impairment; anxiety; feelings of insufficiency; loss of initiative; headache; vertigo. If five of these symptoms occur, a positive diagnosis of KZ Syndrome is made. Symptoms may range from mild to severe, and may manifest immediately or after many years. (4)

Post Traumatic Stress Disorder (PTSD) — diagnosed in earlier periods as war neurosis or shell shock. Now recognized in crime victims, torture survivors, abused children, etc., as well as ex-POWs and veterans. The standard definition, from the Third Edition of the Diagnostic and Statistical Manual:

> The person has experienced an event that is outside
> the range of usual human experience and that
> would be markedly distressing to almost anyone,
> for example, serious threat to one's life or physical
> integrity; serious threat or harm to one's children,
> spouse, or other close relatives and friends; sudden
> destruction of one's home or community; or seeing
> another person who has recently been, or is being,
> seriously injured or killed as the result of an accident
> or physical violence.

> *and*

> The traumatic event is persistently re-experienced.

This re-experiencing might be in the form of dreams or nightmares, flashbacks, or distress in situations that bring to mind the traumatic event. Symptoms of PTSD might include repression of feelings or thoughts related to the trauma, depression, memory loss, loss of interest in significant activities, feelings of detachment, difficulty sleeping, difficulty concentrating, irritability, outbursts of anger, hypervigilance, exaggerated startle response. It is common for symptoms to begin or recur for months or years after the trauma. (5)

Statistically significant service-connected disabilities among former POWs (1946-1979)

WWII Europe	WWII Pacific	Korean Conflict	Vietnam Era
anxiety neurosis	anxiety neurosis	anxiety neurosis	*not available
avitaminosis	avitaminosis	avitaminosis	
arthritis	arthritis	arthritis	
frozen feet residuals	frozen feet residuals	frozen feet residuals	
scars	scars	scars	
	skin diseases	skin diseases	
	beriberi	beriberi	
	malaria	malaria	
	eye diseases	eye diseases	
	respiratory diseases	respiratory diseases	
	gastrointestinal diseases	gastrointestinal diseases	
	genitourinary diseases		
	psychoneurological diseases		
	cardiovascular diseases		

Ranked by the frequency of claims made to the Veterans Administration by former POWs in this period. (10)

*Insufficient data on Vietnam era POWs existed at the time this information was gathered.

References

(1) Clayman, Charles B., MD, editor (1989) *The American Medical Association Encyclopedia of Medicine,* New York: Random House.

(2) Kunz, Jeffrey R.M., MD, editor (1987) *The American Medical Association Family Medical Guide,* New York: Random House.

(3) Larson, David E., MD, editor (1990) *Mayo Clinic Family Health Book,* New York: William Morrow and Company.

(4) Lipton, Merrill I., MD (1988) "Post-Traumatic Stress Disorder in the Older Veteran," reprinted in *Packet 2: Stresses of Incarceration, After-Effects of Extreme Stress,* Arlington, TX: National Medical Research Committee.

(5) Mason, Patrice H.C. (1990). *Recovering from the War,* New York: Random House.

(6) Page, William Frank (1989) "Summary Report of the 1984-85 Questionnaire Study of Former Prisoners of War and Combat Veterans." Report prepared for the Medical Follow-Up Agency of the Institute of Medicine, National Academy of Sciences, Washington D.C.

(7) Ricciardi, J.M., MD (1991) "An Eight-Year Review of 221 Patients with Orthopedic Problems,"*Ex-POW Bulletin,* 48:11.

(8) Shadish, William R., MD (1991) From a speech to the American Ex-POW National Convention in Seattle, WA, Oct. 8, 1990. Reprinted in *Ex-POW Bulletin,* 48:1.

(9) Shadish, William R., MD (1991-1992) From conversations with the author and editor. Expertise drawn from his medical background, from his experience as a POW in the Korean War, and from his position as a member of the National Advisory Committee on Former Prisoners of War.

(10) Skelton, William Paul III, MD (1989). *POW: The American Experiance,* Arlington, TX: National Medical Research Committee.

(11) Sommers, Stan (1980) "The Story of Prisoners of War in Germany," *The European Story,* Arlington, TX: National Medical Research Committee.

(12) Sommers, Stan (1981) "Technical Intelligence Bulletin – Medical," *The Korean Story,* Arlington, TX: National Medical Research Committee.

(13) Walters, John, MD, FRCP (1983) "A Note on My Personal Experience of the Health of Former Far-East Prisoners of War." Paper summarizing clinical data after 30 years treating ex-POWs; also summarizes the Roehampton Report (May 1971) of hepatic disease in ex-POWs. Author served as a Specialist Member of Special F.E.P.O.W. Medical Boards at Exeter, England.

APPENDIX 4
Applying for Compensation and Benefits through the Veterans Administration

If you are a former POW, you may have already used some of the services open to you through the Veterans Administration and the Medical Centers. Depending on your claim, those services might include health care, hospitalization, therapy or counseling, compensation payments, or nursing home care, among others. Many services are free, and former POWs are often accorded priority status in receiving them.

According to VA statistics, however, as many as 30% of former POWs make little or no use of the services offered. If you are one of these "non-utilizers" you should know that the range of benefits available to former POWs has expanded in the past decade. In 1981 Congress passed Public Law 97-37, known as the Former Prisoner of War Act. Under the provisions of the law, a national advisory committee, consisting of medical professionals and former POWs, was formed to assist the Department of Veterans Affairs in matters concerning former POWs. One significant result of these actions has been the VA's introduction of the Comprehensive Medical and Physical Exam, commonly called the POW Protocol Examination. The Veterans Administration also designated coordinators in each VAMC charged with overseeing efforts to meet the health needs of former POWs. Another direct result of PL 97-37 has been to update the list of "presumptive diseases"— those conditions considered service-related for former POWs regardless of evidence documenting the origin of the disease. While the list is still considered incomplete by many, it is a significant improvement over earlier efforts. Continuing research may expand the list in the near future.

These and other changes in the Veterans Administration warrant your attention. If you have received poor medical care or inadequate compensation in the past, you deserve another chance to be fairly examined and treated. Following is an outline of the steps you might follow in applying for VA benefits. Contact the VA Regional Office nearest you (see Appendix 5) for more information. These VA publications may be of use, and can be mailed to you at no cost by the Regional Office in your state:

—Federal Benefits for Veterans and Dependents, IS-1 Fact Sheet, updated January 1991
—A Summary of Department of Veterans Affairs Benefits, VA Pamphlet 27-82-2, revised March 1991

Medical Treatment

To receive medical attention, simply call a Veterans Medical Center or Clinic and request an appointment. For admission to a VA hospital, call the hospital, or have a doctor call on your behalf. Identify yourself as a former POW to receive priority service. Medical service and hospitalization is free to former POWs at all VA medical facilities. Some eye care may be excluded, and dental care is free only to those held captive more than 90 days. Call the VA medical facility nearest you for more information.

Disability Compensation

To apply for compensation for service-connected disability, you must first receive a disability rating. The rating may or may not be coupled with a monthly compensation payment. Both decisions – the rating and the compensation – may be appealed. The entire process can take months or even years and will involve a number of forms.

Don't despair!

Numerous service organizations can help you with this process, as can the Veterans Administration. For example, you might give limited power of attorney to a group such as the American Ex-Prisoners of War, or the VFW, while you prepare your claim for compensation. The power of attorney, limited to only matters involving your claim, will allow an organization to speak on your behalf and gather the information necessary to support your claim. There should be no cost for these services.

These are the steps you will need to follow to apply for a disability rating and compensation:

Application

1 A. Apply for disability rating and compensation through your VA Regional Office

Gather supporting documents, discharge papers, and any medical records supporting your claim

Fill out VA forms from the Regional Office:
- *Applications for Medical Care (POW Exam), VA Form 10-10*
- *Application for Service-Connected Disability, VA Form 21-526*
- *Former POW Medical History Form, VA Form 10-0048*

B. Take a compensation and pension (C & P) medical exam at the nearest VA medical facility

After you file form 21-526, the Regional Office will forward your file to the VA medical facility

The medical facility will call you to set an appointment for the compensation and pension (C & P) exam

Timeframe: expect it to take no more than 30 days from the date you file the application until you are called to set an exam date.

___**2** The medical facility will process your exam results and forward them to the VA Adjudication division, where the Ratings Board will make a determination on your claim.

Timeframe: expect it to take 30-60 days for your exam results to travel from the medical facility to the Ratings Board.

___**3** Ratings Board makes a determination: either denies the claim altogether, or assigns a disability rating and compensation (which can range from $0 a month to thousands for some total disabilities).

Timeframe: the Ratings Board will take 30-60 days to make a determination after they receive your C & P exam results.

___**4** If a compensation is awarded, your first check will arrive about 10 days after you are notified in writing of the determination.

To Appeal

___**1** **If you disagree** with either – or both – the disability rating or compensation award, notify the VA Adjudication division at your Regional Office in writing. They will issue a more thorough explanation of the decision.

___**2** **When you receive the expanded decision**, send the Adjudication division your reasons for appeal. This can be done in a letter, or on a form they might send you. In your response, request an in-person review of your claim, if you desire. This gives you a chance to state your case personally.

Note: you must make your appeal within one year of the Ratings Board decision. After one year, you will need to provide new evidence to reopen the claim.

___**3** **The Ratings Board will now rule on your appeal.** If you are not successful, you can bring your case to the Board of Veterans Appeals. If you are again unsuccessful, you can sue the VA through the Court of Veterans Appeals. This is a relatively new procedure, with unknown effectiveness at this printing. Check with a veterans service organization for advice.

Tips for the Applicant

•Remember that the VA Medical Center and VA Adjudication are separate divisions. Except for your C & P exam, your medical records will *not* be automatically transferred to Adjudication. Attach relevant medical documents to your claims personally.

•In making your original claim, try to gather these kinds of documents:
  – discharge papers
  – medical files from the service period
  – treatment records from shortly after discharge; within one year of discharge is the most effective
  – a continuity of medical treatment for the injury over the years since discharge
  – buddy statements from people who served with you, or witnessed the original injury or subsequent treatment

•Complete all forms carefully and in great detail, but pay special attention to the Former POW Medical History form 10-0048. This form is used by both the Medical Rating Board and the VAMC examining physicians to familiarize them with your POW experience, and assist them in diagnosing your disabilities.

•If you already receive disability compensation and are applying for an increase, you can skip the forms and start by simply making a written request to the Adjudication division.

•Don't be shy about asking for help from a veterans service organization or from the former-POW coordinator in the Veterans Service Division of the VA Regional Office. They are professionals at this, and can make the process easier and quicker for you.

Other Benefits

Veterans Pension – Provides a monthly payment, based on the veteran's current income and net worth. Must be rated 100% permanently and totally disabled. Requires an honorable discharge and wartime service.

Widows Pension – Provides a monthly payment, based on the widow's income and net worth. Awards are not dependent on the veteran's rank or disability, although he must have served during wartime, with an honorable discharge. Payments are made until widow's remarriage and cannot be collected simultaneously with death compensation awards.

Death and Indemnity Compensation – Payments are made monthly to the widow of a veteran whose death or cause of death was service-connected. Awards are based on the veteran's rank, but not on the widow's income or net worth. Payments continue until widow's remarriage.

Family Health Care – CHAMPVA – Civilian Health and Medical Program of the Department of Veterans Affairs. Provides medical care to the spouse or child of a veteran who is rated 100% totally and permanently disabled. Also available if the veteran dies of a service-connected disability, or is rated 100% totally and permanently disabled at the time of death. Provides partial payments of hospital bills and outpatient services.

Presumptive Conditions

Former POWs interned for 30 days or more and suffering from certain diseases do not have to produce military medical records showing that these diseases were incurred or aggravated during active duty or the period of internment. Also, there is no requirement that the first symptoms appear within any specific time period after discharge or separation. If you were interned for 30 days or more and are disabled from any of the diseases listed below to the extent of 10% or more, your disability will be presumed to be service-connected unless there is affirmative evidence of a non service-connected cause.

Following are the conditions currently considered presumptive:

1. *Chronic Dysentery*

2. *Helminthiasis* (worms in the intestines)

3. *Disease of Nutritional Deficiency* including but not limited to beriberi and beriberi heart disease, pellagra, avitaminosis, optic atrophy, malnutrition.

4. *Psychosis* (a mental condition evidenced by a loss of sense of reality)

5. *Any of the Anxiety States* including post traumatic stress disorder. The existence of any of these conditions *should not be cause for embarrassment* for a former POW. Symptoms include being unable to sleep, difficulty in relaxing, nervousness, irritability, constant fatigue, antisocial feeling, nightmares, bad dreams about POW camp days, overeating, and excessive drinking.

6. *Dysthymic Disorder* (or *Depressive Neurosis*) (added by Public Law 98-223, effective October, 1983). Symptoms of this condition include depressed mood (feeling sad, blue, down in the dumps, low) and/or loss of interest in all, or almost all, usual activities and pastimes.

7. *Residuals of Frostbite* (added by Public Law 99-576, effective October, 1986). Only if the Veterans Administration determines veteran was interned in climatic conditions consistent with the occurrence of frostbite.

8. *Post Traumatic Osteoarthritis* (added by Public Law 99-576, effective October, 1986).

9. *Peripheral Neuropathy* (added by Public Law 100-322, effective May, 1988). Except where directly related to infectious causes.

10. *Irritable Bowel Syndrome* (added by Public Law 100-322, effective May, 1988).

11. *Peptic Ulcer Disease*

Further Resources

The National Medical Research Committee of the American Ex-Prisoners of War has put together a very comprehensive booklet on applying for VA compensation. To receive a copy, send $5 plus $1 for shipping, to:

American Ex-Prisoners of War
National Headquarters
3201 E. Pioneer Pkwy, Suite 40
Arlington, Texas 76010

Ask for *Packet 1: VA Claim Information*

APPENDIX 5
Resources to Help the Former POW

Hundreds of organizations stand ready to help the former POW and his family – if only one knows how to find them. In addition to the Veterans Administration, there are service groups, civic groups and veterans groups in every state and territory of the nation. To find out about them, or about legislation and policy affecting veterans, start by calling your state office of Veterans Affairs, listed below. For information about veterans benefits or health service, contact the VA Regional Office or Medical Center nearest you. Those phone numbers are also listed here. Lastly, to connect with national groups of veterans and former POWs, or with their local chapters, start with the organizations listed in these pages. Some of these groups sponsor national reunions, others publish magazines and others conduct continued research into issues affecting the former prisoner of war.

A note about accuracy: wherever feasible, the names of people to contact have been included here for your convenience. All information has been double-checked for accuracy. However, if you are using this guide a year or more after its publication, you may wish to verify the information you plan to use.

STATE DIRECTORS OF VETERANS AFFAIRS

Alabama
Frank D. Wilkes, Director, Department of Veterans Affairs
PO Box 1509, 770 Washington St, Montgomery, Alabama 36102
(205) 242-5077

Alaska
Larry Landry, Director, Division of Veterans Affairs
P.O. Box 5800, Fort Richardson, Alaska 99505
(907) 428-6016

American Samoa
John Tuufala Kane, Director, American Samoa Veterans Affairs
PO Box 8586, Pago Pago, American Somoa 96799
(684) 633-4206

Arizona
Norman O. Gallion, Director, Veterans Service Commission
3225 North Central Ave, Phoenix, Arizona 85012
(602) 255-4713

Arkansas
Hershel W. Gober, Director, Department of Veterans Affairs
PO Box 1280, North Little Rock, Arkansas 72115
(501) 370-3820

California
Benjamin T. Hacker, Director, Department of Veterans Affairs
PO Box 942895, 1227 O St, Sacramento, California 94295
(916) 653-2158

Colorado
Richard F. Ceresko, Director, Division of Veterans Affairs
1575 Sherman St, Denver, Colorado 80203
(303) 866-2494

Connecticut
Hamilton Harper, Commissioner, Department of Veterans Affairs
287 West St, Rocky Hill, Connecticut 06067
(203) 721-5894

Delaware
Antonio Davila, Executive Director, Commission of Veterans Affairs
PO Box 1401, Dover, Delaware 19903
(302) 739-2792

District of Columbia
Thomas Dixon, Jr., Acting Chief, Office of Veterans Affairs
941 N. Capitol St NE, Washington, D.C. 20421
(202) 737-5050

Florida
Earl G. Peck, Director, Department of Veterans Affairs
PO Box 31003, St. Petersburg, Florida 33731
(813) 898-4443

Georgia
Pete Wheeler, Commissioner, Department of Veterans Service
Floyd Veterans Memorial Bldg, Atlanta, Georgia 30334
(404) 656-2300

Guam
John C. Blaz, Administrator, Veterans Affairs Office
PO Box 3279, Agana, Guam 96910
(671) 472-6002

Hawaii
Lawrence S.K. Lee, Director, Office of Veterans Services
733 Bishop St, Honolulu, Hawaii 96813
(808) 587-3010

Idaho
Gary Bermeosolo, Administrator, Division of Veterans Services
PO Box 7765, 320 Collins Rd, Boise, Idaho 83707
(208) 334-5000

Illinois
Robert Poshard, Director, Department of Veterans Affairs
PO Box 19432, 833 S Spring St, Springfield, Illinois 62794
(217) 782-6641

Indiana
Gerald "Dutch" Bole, Director, Department of Veterans Affairs
302 W. Washington St, Indianapolis, Indiana 46204
(317) 232-3910

Iowa
Dale L. Renaud, Administrator, Veterans Affairs Division
7700 NW Beaver Dr, Johnston, Iowa 50131
(515) 242-5333

Kansas
Stan Teasley, Executive Director, Commission on Veterans Affairs
700 SW Jackson, Suite 701, Topeka, Kansas 66603
(913) 296-3976

Kentucky
Larry L. Arnett, Director, Division of Veterans Affairs
Boone National Guard Center, Frankfort, Kentucky 40601
(502) 564-8514

Louisiana
Ernie P. Broussard, Executive Director, Dept. of Veterans Affairs,
PO Box 94095, Capitol Station, Baton Rouge, Louisiana 70804
(504) 922-0500

Maine
Howard E. Eisman, Supervisor, Division of Veterans Services
State House Station 11, Augusta, Maine 04333
(207) 626-4464

Maryland
Clarence M. Bacon, Executive Director, Maryland Veterans
Commission, 31 Hopkins Plaza, Baltimore, Maryland 21201
(301) 962-4700

Massachusetts
Thomas J. Hudner, Jr., Commissioner, Dept. of Veterans Services
Leverett Saltonstall Bldg, Room 1002, Boston, Massachusetts 02202
(617) 727-3570

Michigan
Jack Devine, Director, Veterans Trust Fund
611 W Ottawa St, Lansing, Michigan 48909
(517) 373-3130

Minnesota
Bernie Melter, Commissioner, Department of Veterans Affairs
20 West 12th Street, St. Paul, Minnesota 55155
(612) 296-2562

Mississippi
Jack Stephens, Interim Director, State Veterans Affairs Board
4607 Lindberg Drive, Jackson, Mississippi 39209
(601) 354-7205

Missouri
Robert R. Buckner, Executive Director, Division of Veterans Affairs
1719 Southridge Drive, Jefferson City, Missouri 65102
(314) 751-3343

Montana
Ruddy Reilly, Acting Administrator, Veterans Affairs Division
1100 N Main Street, Helena, Montana 59601
(406) 444-6926

Nebraska
Jonathan F. Sweet, Director, Department of Veterans Affairs
PO Box 95083, State Office Bldg, Lincoln, Nebraska 68509
(402) 471-2458

Nevada
Randy Day, Commissioner, Commission for Veterans Affairs
1201 Terminal Way, Reno, Nevada 89520
(702) 688-1155

New Hampshire
Conrad V. Moran, Director, State Veterans Council
359 Lincoln St, Manchester, New Hampshire 03103
(603) 624-9230

New Jersey
Richard Bernard, Deputy Commissioner, Dept of Military & Veterans Affairs, Eggerts Crossing Rd, CN340, Lawrenceville,
New Jersey 08625
(609) 530-6892

New Mexico
Michael C. D'Arco, Director, Veterans Service Commission
PO Box 2324, Santa Fe, New Mexico 87503
(505) 827-6300

New York
James R. Peluso, Director, Division of Veterans Affairs
Corning Tower, 28th Floor, Albany, New York 12223
(518) 474-3752

North Carolina
Charles F. Smith, Assistant Secretary, Division of Veterans Affairs
325 N Salisbury St, Raleigh, North Carolina 27603
(919) 733-3851

North Dakota
Milton W. Kane, Commissioner, North Dakota Department of
Veterans Affairs, PO Box 9003, Fargo, North Dakota 58106
(701) 239-7165

Ohio
David E. Aldstadt, Director, Governor's Office of Veterans Affairs
30 E Broad Street, Room 1825, Columbus, Ohio 43266
(614) 466-5453

Oklahoma
Richard P. Heuckendorf, Director, Department of Veterans Affairs
2311 N Central, Oklahoma City, Oklahoma 73152
(405) 521-3684

Oregon
Jon A. Mangis, Director, Department of Veterans Affairs
700 Summer St NE, Salem, Oregon 97310
(503) 373-2000

Pennsylvania
Joseph R. Clelan, Director, Bureau for Veterans Affairs
Fort Indiantown Gap, Annville, Pennsylvania 17003
(717) 865-8901

Puerto Rico
Rogel Orfila Barreto, Public Advocate for Veterans Affairs
1603 Ponce DeLeon Ave, Santurce, Puerto Rico 00909
(809) 725-4400

Rhode Island
David C. Foehr, Chief, Veterans Affairs Office
Metacom Ave, Bristol, Rhode Island 02809
(401) 277-2488

South Carolina
Bill J. Sams, Director, Department of Veterans Affairs
1205 Pendleton St, Columbia, South Carolina 29201
(803) 734-0200

South Dakota
Dennis G. Foell, Director, Division of Veterans Affairs
c/o 500 E. Capitol Ave, Pierre, South Dakota 57501
(605) 773-4981

Tennessee
W.D. (Bill) Manning, Commissioner, Department of Veterans Affairs, 215 8th Ave N, Nashville, Tennessee 37243
(615) 741-2345

Texas
Douglas K. Brown, Executive Director, Texas Veterans Commission
E.O. Thompson Bldg, 10th and Colorado St, Austin, Texas 78701
(512) 463-5538

Utah
Jerry Gessner, Veterans Services Officer, Dept. of Veteran Affairs
125 S State Street, Salt Lake City, Utah 84147
(801) 524-5960
* This is the federal Regional Office; no state division exists.

Vermont
Aline (Lyn) Boisjoli, Co-director, Veterans Affairs Office
120 State St, Montpelier, Vermont 05620
(802) 828-3379

Virgin Islands
Verne I. Richards, Director, Division of Veterans Affairs
22 Hospital St, Christiansted, St. Croix, Virgin Islands 00820
(809) 773-6663

Virginia
Rick O'Dell, Director, Department of Veterans Affairs
210 Franklin Rd SW, PO Box 809, Roanoke, Virginia 24004
(703) 982-6396

Washington
Jesse Farias, Director, Department of Veterans Affairs
505 E Union, Olympia, Washington 98504
(206) 753-5586

West Virginia
G.L. Harper, Director, Division of Veterans Affairs
1321 Plaza East, Charleston, West Virginia 25301
(304) 348-3661

Wisconsin
Raymond G. Boland, Secretary, Department of Veterans Affairs
30 W Mifflin Street, Madison, Wisconsin 53703
(608) 266-1311

Wyoming
Robert Landes, Chairman, Veterans Affairs Commission
622 Ridgeland St, Cheyenne, Wyoming 82009
(307) 777-6069

VA FACILITIES

Alabama
Medical Centers: Birmingham (205) 933-8101; Montgomery
(205) 272-4670; Tuscaloosa (205) 554-2000; Tuskegee (205) 727-0550
Clinic: Mobile (205) 690-2875
Regional Office: 1-800-392-8054

Alaska
Clinics: Anchorage (800) 478-4400; Fort Wainwright (907) 353-5208
Regional Office: 1-800-478-2500

Arizona
Medical Centers: Phoenix (602) 277-5551; Prescott (602) 445-4860;
Tucson (602) 792-1450
Regional Office: 1-800-827-2031

Arkansas
Medical Centers: Fayetteville (501) 443-4301; Little Rock
(501) 661-1202
Regional Office: 1-800-827-2033

California
Medical Centers: Fresno (209) 225-6100; Livermore (415) 447-2560;
Loma Linda (714) 825-7084; Long Beach (213) 494-2611; Martinez
(510) 372-2000; Palo Alto (415) 493-5000; San Diego (619) 552-8585;
San Francisco (415) 221-4810; Sepulveda (818) 891-7711; West
Los Angeles (213) 478-3711
Clinics: Los Angeles (213) 894-3902; Oakland (415) 273-7096;
Sacramento (916) 440-2625; San Diego (619) 557-6210; Santa Barbara
(805) 683-1491
Regional Offices: Los Angeles 1-800-827-2013; San Diego
1-800-532-3811; San Francisco 1-800-827-0641

Colorado
Medical Centers: Denver (303) 399-8020; Fort Lyon (719) 456-1260;
Grand Junction (303) 242-0731
Clinic: Colorado Springs (719) 380-0004
Regional Office: 1-800-332-6742

Connecticut
Medical Centers: Newington (203) 666-6951; West Haven (203)
932-5711
Regional Office: 1-800-842-4315

Delaware
Medical Center: Wilmington (302) 994-2511
Regional Office: 1-800-292-7855

District of Columbia
Medical Center: Washington, DC (202) 745-8000
Regional Office: (202) 872-1151

Florida
Medical Centers: Bay Pines (813) 398-6661; Gainesville
(904) 376-1611; Lake City (904) 755-3016; Miami (305) 324-4455;
Tampa (813) 972-2000
Clinics: Daytona Beach (904) 274-4600; Fort Myers (813) 939-3939;
Jacksonville (904) 791-2751; Oakland Park (305) 771-2101;
Orlando (407) 425-7521; Pensacola (904) 476-1100; Port Richey
(813) 869-3203; Riviera Beach (407) 845-2800
Regional Office: 1-800-827-2204

Georgia
Medical Centers: Augusta (404) 733-0188; Decatur (404) 321-6111;
Dublin (912) 272-1210
Regional Office: 1-800-282-0232

Hawaii
Clinic: Honolulu (808) 541-1600
Regional Office: 1-800-232-2535

Idaho
Medical Center: Boise (208) 336-5100
Regional Office: 1-800-632-2003

Illinois
Medical Centers: Chicago (Lakeside) (312) 943-8247; Chicago
(Westside) (312) 666-6500; Danville (217) 442-8000; Hines (708)
343-7200; Marion (618) 997-5311; North Chicago (708) 688-1900
Clinic: Peoria (309) 671-7350
Regional Office: 1-800-827-0466

Indiana
Medical Centers: Fort Wayne (219) 426-5431; Indianapolis (317)
635-7401; Marion (317) 674-3321
Clinics: Crown Point (219) 662-0001; Evansville (812) 465-6202
Regional Office: 1-800-827-0634

Iowa
Medical Centers: Des Moines (515) 255-2173; Iowa City
(319) 338-0581; Knoxville (515) 842-3101
Regional Office: 1-800-362-2222

Kansas
Medical Centers: Leavenworth (913) 682-2000; Topeka
(913) 272-3111; Wichita (316) 685-2221
Regional Office: 1-800-827-0445

Kentucky
Medical Centers: Lexington (606) 233-4511; Louisville (502) 895-3401
Regional Office: 1-800-827-2050

Louisiana
Medical Centers: Alexandria (318) 473-0010; New Orleans
(504) 568-0811; Shreveport (318) 221-8411
Regional Office: 1-800-462-9510

Maine
Medical Center: Togus (207) 623-8411
Regional Office: 1-800-452-1935

Maryland
Medical Centers: Baltimore (301) 467-9932; Fort Howard
(301) 477-1800; Perry Point (301) 642-2411
Clinic: Baltimore (301) 962-4610
Regional Office: 1-800-492-9503

Massachusetts
Medical Centers: Bedford (617) 275-7500; Boston (617) 232-9500;
Brockton (508) 583-4500; Northampton (413) 584-4040;
West Roxbury (617) 323-7700
Clinics: Boston (617) 248-1000; Lowell (508) 453-1746; Springfield
(413) 785-0301; New Bedford (508) 999-5504; Worcester (508) 793-0200
Regional Office: 1-800-392-6015

Michigan
Medical Centers: Allen Park (313) 562-6000; Ann Arbor
(313) 769-7100; Battle Creek (616) 966-5600; Iron Mountain
(906) 774-3300; Saginaw (517) 793-2340
Clinics: Gaylord (517) 732-7525; Grand Rapids (616) 459-2200
Regional Office: 1-800-827-1996

Minnesota
Medical Centers: Minneapolis (612) 725-2000; St. Cloud
(612) 252-1670
Regional Office: 1-800-422-8079

Mississippi
Medical Centers: Biloxi (601) 388-5541; Jackson (601) 362-4471
Regional Office: 1-800-827-2028

Missouri
Medical Centers: Columbia (314) 443-2511; Kansas City (816) 861-4700;
Poplar Bluff (314) 686-4151; St. Louis (John Cochran Div.)
(314) 652-4100; St. Louis (Jefferson Barracks Div.) (314) 487-0400
Regional Office: 1-800-392-3761

Montana
Medical Centers: Fort Harrison (406) 442-6410; Miles City (406) 232-3060
Clinic: Billings (406) 657-6786
Regional Office: 1-800-332-6125

Nebraska
Medical Centers: Grand Island (308) 382-3660; Lincoln (402) 489-3802; Omaha (402) 346-8800
Regional Office: 1-800-827-6544

Nevada
Medical Center: Reno (702) 786-7200
Clinic: Las Vegas (702) 385-3700
Regional Office: 1-800-992-5740

New Hampshire
Medical Center: Manchester (603) 624-4366
Regional Office: 1-800-562-5260

New Jersey
Medical Centers: East Orange (908) 676-1000; Lyons (201) 647-0180
Regional Office: 1-800-242-5867

New Mexico
Medical Center: Albuquerque (505) 265-1711
Regional Office: 1-800-432-6853

New York
Medical Centers: Albany (518) 462-3311; Batavia (716) 343-7500; Bath (607) 776-2111; Bronx (212) 584-9000; Brooklyn (718) 630-3500; Buffalo (716) 834-9200; Canandaigua (716) 394-2000; Castle Point (914) 831-2000; Montrose (914) 737-4400; New York City (212) 686-7500; Northport (516) 261-4400; Syracuse (315) 476-7461
Clinics: Brooklyn (212) 330-7785; New York City (212) 620-6636; Rochester (716) 263-5734
Regional Office: Buffalo 1-800-827-0619; New York City 1-800-827-8954

North Carolina
Medical Centers: Asheville (704) 298-7911; Durham (919) 286-0411; Fayetteville (919) 488-2120; Salisbury (704) 638-9000
Clinic: Winston-Salem (919) 631-5562
Regional Office: 1-800-642-0841

North Dakota
Medical Center: Fargo (701) 232-3241
Regional Office: 1-800-342-4790

Ohio

Medical Centers: Brecksville (216) 526-3030; Chillicothe
(614) 773-1141; Cincinnati (513) 861-3100; Cleveland (216) 791-3800;
Dayton (513) 268-6511
Clinics: Canton (216) 489-4660; Columbus (614) 469-5665; Toledo
(419) 259-2000
Regional Office: 1-800-827-8272

Oklahoma

Medical Centers: Muskogee (918) 683-3261; Oklahoma City
(405) 270-0501
Clinic: Tulsa (918) 581-7152
Regional Office: 1-800-827-2206

Oregon

Medical Centers: Portland (503) 220-8262; Roseburg (503) 440-1000
Clinic: Portland (503) 244-9222
Regional Office: 1-800-452-7276

Pennsylvania

Medical Centers: Altoona (814) 943-8164; Butler (412) 287-4781;
Coatesville (215) 384-7711; Erie (814) 868-8661; Lebanon
(717) 272-6621; Philadelphia (215) 823-5800; Pittsburgh (University
Drive C) (412) 692-3000; Pittsburgh (Highland Dr) (412) 363-4900;
Wilkes-Barre (717) 824-2521
Clinics: Allentown (215) 776-4304; Harrisburg (717) 782-4590;
Philadelphia (215) 597-7244; Sayre (717) 888-8062
Regional Offices: Philadelphia 1-800-869-8387; Pittsburgh
1-800-242-0233

Philippines

Regional Office: Manila, local, 810-521-7116; from U.S., 011632
521-7116

Puerto Rico

Medical Center: San Juan (809) 758-7575
Clinic: Mayaguez (809) 831-3400
Regional Office: from the island, 1-800-462-4135; from U.S. Virgin
Islands, 1-800-474-2976

Rhode Island

Medical Center: Providence (401) 457-3042
Regional Office: 1-800-322-0230

South Carolina

Medical Centers: Charleston (803) 577-5011; Columbia (803) 776-4000
Clinic: Greenville (803) 232-7303
Regional Office: 1-800-922-1000

South Dakota
Medical Centers: Fort Meade (605) 347-2511; Hot Springs
(605) 745-2000; Sioux Falls (605) 336-3230
Regional Office: 1-800-952-3550

Tennessee
Medical Centers: Memphis (901) 523-8990; Mountain Home (615)
926-1171; Murfreesboro (615) 893-1360; Nashville (615) 327-4751
Clinics: Chattanooga (615) 855-6550; Knoxville (615) 549-9319
Regional Office: 1-800-342-8330

Texas
Medical Centers: Amarillo (806) 355-9703; Big Spring (915) 263-7361;
Bonham (903) 583-2111; Dallas (214) 376-5451; Houston
(713) 791-1414; Kerrville (512) 896-2020; Marlin (817) 883-3511;
San Antonio (512) 617-5300; Temple (817) 778-4811; Waco
(817) 752-6581
Clinics: Beaumont (409) 839-2480; Corpus Christi (512) 888-3251;
El Paso (915) 541-7811; Lubbock (806) 743-7219; McAllen
(512) 682-4581; San Antonio (512) 641-2672
Regional Offices: Houston 1-800-827-2021; Waco 1-800-792-3271

Utah
Medical Center: Salt Lake City (801) 582-1565
Regional Office: 1-800-662-9163

Vermont
Medical Center: White River Junction (802) 295-9363
Regional Office: 1-800-622-4134

Virginia
Medical Centers: Hampton (804) 722-9961; Richmond (804) 230-0001;
Salem (703) 982-2463
Regional Office: 1-800-827-2018

Washington
Medical Centers: Seattle (206) 762-1010; Spokane (509) 328-4521;
Tacoma (206) 582-8440; Walla Walla (509) 525-5200
Regional Office: 1-800-827-0638

West Virginia
Medical Centers: Beckley (304) 255-2121; Clarksburg (304) 623-3461;
Huntington (304) 429-6741; Martinsburg (304) 263-0811
Regional Office: 1-800-827-2052

Wisconsin
Medical Centers: Madison (608) 256-1901; Milwaukee (414) 384-2000;
Tomah (608) 372-3971
Clinic: Superior (715) 392-9711
Regional Office: 1-800-827-0464

Wyoming
Medical Centers: Cheyenne (307) 778-7550; Sheridan (307) 672-3473
Regional Office: 1-800-442-2761

NATIONAL VETERAN AND EX-POW GROUPS

American Defenders of Bataan and Corregidor
Elmer E. Long, Jr., National Secretary
PO Box 12052
New Burn, North Carolina 28561-2052
(919) 637-4033

American Ex-Prisoners of War — National Headquarters
Clydie Morgan, National Adjutant
3201 E Pioneer Pkwy, Suite 40
Arlington, Texas 76010
(817) 649-2979

American Ex-Prisoners of War — National Medical Research
Committee
Albert Bland, Chairman
738 Joppa Farm Road
Joppa, Maryland 21085
(410) 679-4103

The American Legion — Washington Office
John Sommer, Jr., Director
1608 K St NW
Washington DC 20006
(202) 861-2700

AMVETS — National Headquarters
Noel C. Woosley, National Service and Legislative Director
4647 Forbes Blvd
Lanham, Maryland 20706
(301) 459-9600

Disabled American Veterans — National Headquarters
Charles E. Joeckel, Jr., National Adjutant
807 Maine Ave SW
Washington DC 20024
(202) 554-3501

Military Order of the Purple Heart — National Headquarters
Gregory A. Bresser, National Service Director
5413-B Backlick Rd
Springfield, Virginia 22151-3960
(703) 642-5360

NAM-POWs
Robert Doremus, National Secretary
2757 Elm Ave
Bexley, Ohio 43209

Survivors of Wake, Guam and Cavite
Max Boesiger, President
PO Box 1241
Boise, Idaho 83702
(208) 375-6239

Veterans of Foreign Wars — Washington Office
Larry W. Rivers, Executive Director
200 Maryland Ave NE
Washington DC 20002
(202) 543-2239

APPENDIX 6
Recommendations to Help Ex-POWS

There were fewer than 69,000 American ex-POWs still alive in January, 1992. Nearly 63,000 of them are veterans of World War II. Many of these aging, presumably ill ex-POWs are not active in veterans organizations, and a significant number have never filed a claim for compensation with the Veterans Administration. Why? Is it because they don't need help? More likely, it's because not enough has been done to reach this very isolated group of veterans. Or because they don't believe that participation will yield benefits worthy of the extreme personal cost of asking for help. Following are some suggestions, both for reaching these disabled veterans, and for helping them when we do.

Veteran's Organizations

1. Increase Outreach

Veterans organizations exist for the purpose of helping those who cannot help themselves. Every group would do well to establish measuring devices to chart their progress in those kinds of helping activities. One part of that program would consist of a recruiting campaign to expand membership. There may be a number of reasons why ex-prisoners of war do not belong to such groups. More than likely, these men stay away because they suffer from post traumatic stress disorder. They are afraid of the emotional pain they will suffer if they expose themselves to meetings with people who discuss subjects they have been trying to avoid for so long. It will take persistent and patient one-on-one persuasion by individual members to bring these men into participation in veterans organizations.

2. Maintain Support Groups

If your local veterans organization does not already provide a support group for ex-POWs, now is the time to establish one. Sometimes the only way these veterans can get help is by opening up with each other first. Support groups should be regular, well-publicized, and require no long-term commitment to attend. If possible, they should be facilitated by a mental health professional with expertise in the problems of ex-POWs. However, even an informal self-help group can provide relief. Support groups for spouses and children of ex-POWs would also help.

3. Work to Improve Disability Ratings

Too many former prisoners of war are vastly underrated in the percentage of disability awarded to them by the DVA. No veterans group has demonstrated concern about that problem as an organization. It would seem that a first step would be to appoint a task force to make specific recommendations to put into effect a program to improve disability ratings. We have so much talent, experience, and influence among our members that we should be able to find the answers if we make a sustained effort to do so.

4. Recommend Specific Mental Health Professionals

One of the short-term steps an organization can take is to prepare a roster of mental health professionals, especially psychiatrists, employed by the VA who are competent to deal with the ex-POW. These doctors must have provided evidence that they believe in post traumatic stress disorder as a valid diagnosis of mental illness, and that they recognize it as a chronic condition in former prisoners of war. Then we must insist that all of our ex-POW comrades receive their psychiatric evaluation *only* from one of the doctors whose name appears on the list. If such a person is not available in the area where the ex-POW resides, then the VA must be brought to understand that they are obligated to transport the doctor to the patient or the patient to the doctor that he has selected to make the evaluation.

5. Employ Advocates

Veterans organizations need to employ advocates to represent those patients who are too sick (disturbed) to make use of the VA system and too disabled to do the paperwork and the interviews that are needed to process an application for a disability rating. While many of our ex-POW members are physically disabled, the majority of our members suffer from psychological impairments first and in far greater proportions. It is also true that the degree of impairment, mentally or psychologically, is inverse in proportion to the amount of assistance received from the DVA system. Those who are the most disabled are those whose disability makes it extremely unlikely that they will be able to muster the will power and the determination to make a proper case for themselves and see it through despite all the bureaucratic obstacles they may encounter.

6. Sponsor Research

Research is needed to establish a mental health category for the illnesses which follow prolonged periods of incarceration in prisons and concentration camps. As noted elsewhere in these essays, PTSD as a diagnosis is only partially applicable, as it describes the response to single traumas of unusual intensity. Former prisoners of war suffered many traumas and for longer periods of time than the soldiers originally diagnosed with PTSD. Further, little is yet known about the long-term physical effects of disease and malnutrition. In this connection, follow-up studies should be conducted with the survivors of the prison camps.

Families of Ex-POWS

1. Attend Therapy

Spouses and children of ex-POWs can learn to cope and reduce stress by attending group therapy sessions, taking part in couple therapy, and seeking individual therapy.

2. Encourage Protocol Exams

Families should encourage the ex-POW to come in to the VA Medical Center for their protocol physical examination, which the VA is obligated to give. This is not easy for the ex-POW to do, but it is an essential step to proper diagnosis and treatment. When the ex-POW dies, the family should ask for an autopsy to determine exact cause of death and the extent of physical damage from imprisonment experiences.

3. Insist on Preferred Mental Health Professionals
Families should insist the ex-POW be examined by mental health professionals who are familiar with the problems of PTSD, and who will be willing to look for hidden signs of PTSD and chronic depression.

4. Insist on Full Examinations
The ex-POW needs to know that he is entitled to one full hour in the psychiatric part of the exam. It takes a good psychiatrist at least that long to break through defenses and establish a dialogue of trust. If the ex-POW is dismissed after only 15 minutes, he is entitled to have this part of the exam rescheduled.

5. Get Involved
Families of ex-POWs need to get more involved in local ex-POW organizations. There are benefits for disabled veterans and eligibility requirements that families need to understand. Further, because many ex-POWs suffer from hearing loss, they do not understand much of what is said at chapter meetings. Family attendance at meetings can bridge the communication gap.

Ex-POWS

1. Attend Local Meetings
Now is the time to get involved in your local veterans organization. If you feel out of place for any reason, bring a friend who understands, or try another group. Don't give up!

2. Stand Up For Your Rights
Whatever group you attend, participate in political or lobbying efforts to improve the lot of the disabled veteran. You are stronger in a group. On an individual level, register complaints whenever it is appropriate. Do not let poor treatment or poorly trained staff go unnoticed. If enough voices are heard, change will come about.

3. Consider Group Therapy
There is never any commitment or obligation to say more than you want. You can sit quietly, or leave the room at any time. It won't relieve all your problems, but you may find you sleep better, or have fewer nightmares, or feel less depressed. It's worth the initial discomfort to reap those benefits.

4. Take Your Protocol Exam
Insist on your full medical and psychiatric evaluation, and by a doctor who knows the symptoms of PTSD. Report inappropriate remarks or unprofessional conduct by VAMC staff. Contest the results if you feel an exam was incomplete or unfair.

5. Maintain Your Health

You may not like to admit it, but your health must have been adversely affected by the prison camp experience. You must see the doctor regularly and document your illnesses and symptoms. Use the VA medical centers whenever possible to save your family the medical expense.

6. Talk to Your Family

They are the people who care most about you. Tell them when things are hard for you, or when you need help. Don't shut them out! You needn't share details of your past that are uncomfortable, but you owe them as much attention now as you can muster. Things are harder for your family when you don't let them in.

An Agenda for Change

These things must be accomplished if ex-POWs and their families are going to receive the treatment they need and deserve. Some are policy changes, to be implemented by individual veterans facilities. Others will require legislative action. It is important to remember that bad policy is a result of human error and ignorance. And good policy results only from human effort and commitment. Each of us must do what we can to change things for the better.

1. Train VA Psychiatrists in PTSD

As noted above, it is imperative that former prisoners of war be evaluated by psychiatrists familiar with their condition and the long-term effects of PTSD. Such a roster should be created for each VAMC; those centers with no qualified psychiatrist should begin the appropriate training/recruiting now.

2. Compensate Widows Fairly

The current system compensates widows of ex-POWs according to the rank their husbands held on discharge. But rank has no bearing on injury, particularly when one considers the psychological effects of PTSD. In general, widows have spent a lifetime providing unpaid nursing services to their traumatized spouses. Not only have their own earning power and social security benefits been curtailed, but their husband's lifetime earnings are likely to have been far below their potential. Additionally, widows usually have enormous medical bills to pay, both for themselves and for husbands who would not or could not get adequate treatment at government medical facilities.

3. Restructure Disability Rating System

The current system for rating disabilities is unfair and inefficient. It is widely known that the same evidence of disability can result in a rating of zero in one state and 100% in another. It's no wonder ex-POWs don't trust this system! Compensation must be restructured in two ways:

> 1. The rating system must be uniform throughout the nation, applied efficiently, clearly and without bias.

2. The system must incorporate new research and evidence of the long-term effects of PTSD on emotional, physical and psychological health. Interviewers must be trained to search for the symptoms, as the ex-POW may not be able to discuss them freely. Eligibility should be uniformly expanded to include psychological trauma as evidenced by poor work performance, strained family relationships, and chronic depression. New credence should also be given to the long-term effects of starvation on the body's skeletal structure, neuropathy and digestive health.

4. Implement Minimum Disability Compensation

No ex-POW should ever be rated at zero percent disability. It is unthinkable that their experiences in brutal captivity would have no effects on long-term health and earning power. A minimum rating of 50% for all former prisoners of war should be immediately implemented to counter the inability of most to apply for just ratings. This is the least our government can offer these injured veterans.

5. Renew Commitment to Disabled Veterans

Veterans organizations throughout the nation must take a two-pronged approach to their problem of credibility with disabled veterans. First, they must double efforts at outreach to these isolated veterans. Second, they must implement new standards for training their staff, with an emphasis on the behavioral characteristics specific to ex-POWs, and on sensitivity in dealing with them.

6. Push for National Recognition

Former prisoners of war are truly the forgotten veterans. Nationally, we must continue to encourage legislation on their behalf. Internationally, the United States must take a firm stand in demanding an apology and/or remuneration from aggressor countries that mistreated American service personnel and civilians during wartime.

APPENDIX 7
Bibliography

*Hundreds of books and articles have been written about the POW experience. Following is a selected bibliography, chosen on the basis of recommendations by others. Many of these books are now out of print, available only through the library or used book stores. The * denotes some of the selections currently available in the Patients Library at the Madison, Wisconsin, Veterans Administration Medical Center. This collection is maintained through the efforts and donations of volunteers, patients, and staff.*

Diary/Memoir

Vietnam

Beyond Survival: Building on the Hard Times – A POW's Inspiring Story, Gerald Coffee (1990). New York: GP Putnam's Sons. First-hand account of Coffee's seven years in captivity and the spiritual lessons he now lives by as a result. Also available on audio cassette.

Chained Eagle, Everett Alvarez, Jr., and Anthony S. Pitch (1989). New York: Donald J. Fine Inc. The first American shot down over North Vietnam, Alvarez endured 8 1/2 years of imprisonment before returning home a hero. Written in the first-person, with photos.

Five Years to Freedom, Major James N. Rowe (1970). Boston: Little Brown and Company. Captured in 1963 by the Viet Cong, Rowe was held until his escape in 1968. Written from his diaries, illustrated with drawings and photos.

The Hanoi Commitment, James Mulligan (1981). Virginia Beach, VA: RIF Marketing. Detailed account of Captain Mulligan's seven years of captivity, including 42 months in solitary confinement.*

In Love and War: The Story of a Family's Ordeal and Sacrifice During the Vietnam Years, James and Sybil Stockdale (1975). New York: Harper & Row. The first-person story of James Stockdale, the highest ranking American POW held in Vietnam. Tells of his 7 1/2 years in the Hanoi prison camp, his family's experiences, and the years immediately after his release.*

In the Presence of Mine Enemies, Howard and Phyllis Rutledge, with Mel and Lyla White (1973). Old Tappan, NJ: Fleming H. Revell Company. The story of Rutledge's capture and seven years as a prisoner of the North Vietnamese. Told first from his perspective, then from the perspective of his wife Phyllis.

The Passing of the Night, Robinson Risner (1973). New York: Random House. Robinson's seven years as a prisoner of the North Vietnamese; told with a unique focus on the moments of joy and humor he discovered in each day, and the reaffirmation of his spirituality and patriotism.

We Came to Help, Monika Schwinn and Bernhard Diehl (1973). New York: Harcourt Brace Jovanovich. The story of two German nurses captured and held by the North Vietnamese more than four years. Gives a different view of the American prisoners and their captors.

Yet Another Voice, Norman A. McDaniel (1975). New York: Hawthorn Books. First-hand account of the author's seven years in North Vietnamese hands. More than half of his book describes his adjustment to life after his release.

Korea

Believed to Be Alive, John W. Thornton (1981). Middlebury, VT: Paul S. Eriksson Publishers. The Navy pilot's first-hand account of his capture and three years as a POW in the Korean War, including the Koreans' attempts at brainwashing.

The Endless Hours, Wallace L. Brown (1961). New York: WW Norton & Company. The story of Wallace's 2 1/2 years as a prisoner in Chinese communist prisons, after being shot down on a mission over North Korea.

General Dean's Story, William F. Dean and William L. Wordon (1954). New York: The Viking Press. First-hand account of the General's three years in captivity behind Korean lines.

I Should Have Died, Philip Deane (1977). New York: Atheneum. The Korean War from another perspective. The son of a Greek military hero, Deane was a journalist for the British when he was captured in Korea. After resisting brainwashing for three years, Deane was released, only to find himself in agreement with the tenets of communism in the second half of his life.

Reactionary! Lloyd W. Pate and B.J. Cutler (1955). New York: Harper & Brothers. Detailed account of the brainwashing methods and torture inflicted on Pate, branded a reactionary by the North Koreans for his refusal to cooperate.

Valley of the Shadow, Ward M. Millar (1955). New York: David McKay Company. Remarkable story of Millar's escape from a Korean prison camp – using hand-made "crawling boards" to compensate for two broken ankles.

A Crowd is Not Company, Robert Kee (1947). London: Jonathan Cape Publishers. A narrative account of the author's three years as a British prisoner of war in Germany.

Bamboo Doctor, Stanley S. Pavillard (1960). New York: MacMillan & Co. The fall of Singapore through Dr. Pavillard's eyes, followed by his 3 1/2 years as a prisoner of war, struggling to save lives with hand-made medical equipment and no medicine.

Behind Japanese Lines: An American Guerrilla in the Philippines, Ray C. Hunt and Bernard Norling (1986). Lexington, KY: The University Press of Kentucky. First-person account of Ray Hunt's escape from the Bataan Death March and three years as a guerrilla in the Filipinos' fight against the Japanese.

Forbidden Diary: A Record of Wartime Internment, 1941-1945, Natalie Crouter (1980). New York: Burt Franklin & Co. The journals of an American civilian woman, her husband and two children, held in Luzon during World War II.

Forbidden Family: A Wartime Memoir of the Philippines, Margaret Sams, edited by Lynn Z. Bloom (1989). Madison, WI: University of Wisconsin Press. A memoir of Margaret Sams, interned by the Japanese, and her camp romance with a fellow internee.

The Hotel Tacloban, Douglas Valentine (1984). Westport, CT: Lawrence Hill & Co. The experiences of Douglas Valentine, Sr., held in a little-known Japanese camp in the Philippines, and of the U.S. military cover-up that followed his release.

Lieutenant Ramsey's War, Edwin Price Ramsey and Stephen J. Rivele (1990). New York: Knightsbridge Publishing Company. The story of Edwin Ramsey, who escaped the Bataan Death March and became instead the leader of 40,000 Filipino guerrillas fighting against the Japanese.

The Ordeal of Elizabeth Vaughan: A Wartime Diary of the Philippines, Carol M. Petillo, editor (1985). University of Georgia Press. Diaries of civilian Vaughan, interned three years with her two children after the fall of Corregidor.

Philippine War Diary: 1939-1945, Stephen Mellnik (1981). New York: Van Nostrand Reinhold Company. Reconstructed from diary fragments and interviews; Mellnik tells about the last days of Corregidor and Bataan, his own capture by the Japanese, and the year he spent in Davao Penal Colony. Mellnik escaped and spent two years assisting the Philippine guerrilla forces before finding his way back to the United States in 1944.

Return to Freedom, Samuel C. Grashio and Bernard Norling (1982). Tulsa, OK: MCN Press. Samuel Grashio's story as a survivor of the Bataan Death March, a prisoner in three Japanese camps, and one of 12 men who engineered the only known mass escape from the Japanese.*

Some Survived: An Epic Account of Japanese Captivity During WWII, Manny Lawton (1984). North Carolina: Algonquin Books of Chapel Hill. An eyewitness account of the Bataan Death March and more than two years of slave labor in Japanese camps.*

Non-fiction

Vietnam

The Heroes Who Fell from Grace, Charles J. Patterson and G. Lee Tippin (1985). Canton, OH: Daring Books. Recounts Operation Lazurus, the failed attempt by the United States to free American POWs believed still held in Laos in 1982.

Bouncing Back: How a Heroic Band of POWs Survived Vietnam, Geoffrey Norman (1990). Boston: Houghton Mifflin Co. The story of Al Stafford, a navy pilot held six years as a POW. "Bouncing back" is the military term now given to the survival tactics developed by Stafford and his fellow prisoners.

Conversations with the Enemy: The Story of PFC Robert Garwood, Winston Groom and Duncan Spencer (1983). New York: GP Putnam's Sons. Controversial and challenging – the story of Bobby Garwood who entered prison camp at age 18 and returned to the United States 14 years later – to charges of treason and consorting with the enemy.*

POW: A Definitive History of the American Prisoner of War Experience in Vietnam, 1964-1973, John Hubbell (1976). New York: McGraw-Hill. Constructed from interviews with more than 200 former POWs. A chronological treatment of events from 1964 when Everett Alvarez, Jr. was captured, to the 1973 signing of the Paris peace agreements.

Prisoner at War: The Survival of Commander Richard A. Stratton, Scott Blakey (1978). New York: Anchor Press/Doubleday. Chronicles Stratton's six years as a prisoner of war of the North Vietnamese from three perspectives: Stratton's struggle as the POW, his wife Alice's ordeal to raise their family alone, and his sister Ellen's anti-war activism.

Survivors, Zalin Grant (1975). New York: WW Norton & Company. Compiled from interviews of nine Americans held prisoner for five years, first in a Viet Cong jungle camp, then in Hanoi. Uses their stories to give a cross-section of experiences, revealing a broader view of the POW's life.*

Vietnam Veterans: The Road to Recovery, Joel Osler Brende and Erwin Randolph Parson (1985). New York: Plenum Press. Useful for all veterans and their families. Authors look at the healing process for Vietnam veterans, including reuniting with families, dealing with suppressed combat experiences, and fitting into society again. Extensive chapter on PTSD; another chapter on overcoming obstacles to seeking psychological counseling.

Korea

Beyond Courage, Clay Blair Jr. (1955). New York: David McKay Company. Stories of Air Force pilots who evaded capture or escaped from prison camps during the Korean War.

The Captives of Korea: An Unofficial White Paper, William L. White (1957). New York: Charles Scribner's Sons. The treatment by the Koreans of American POWs, contrasted with U.S. treatment of Korean POWs. Includes this interesting statistic: while 21 American POWs succumbed to brainwashing and joined their captors' cause, 88,000 Korean POWs rebelled against their return home – won over by the food, housing and educational opportunities in the American prison camps.*

In Every War But One, Eugene Kinkead (1959). New York: WW Norton & Co. Based on a five-year study by the Army of the effect of indoctrination on Americans held by the Koreans. Raises disturbing questions about the conduct of United States soldiers in captivity, and about Korean treatment of the POWs.

World War II

A Sinister Twilight: The Fall of Singapore, 1942, Noel Barber (1968). Boston: Houghton Mifflin Company. Detailed description of the 70 days of Japanese attacks and subsequent fall of Singapore, told from a civilian perspective.

Colditz: The Full Story, P.R. Reid (1984). New York: St. Martin's Press. Germany's answer to recaptured escapees from other camps. Recounted by an escapee from Colditz, with diaries, maps, photos and interviews of other ex-inmates.

Colditz: The Great Escapes, Ron Baybutt (1982). Boston: Little Brown and Company. Collection of authentic German photographs documenting successful and unsuccessful escape attempts from Germany's most secure POW camp.*

Corregidor: The End of the Line, Eric Morris (1981). New York: Stein and Day Publishers. The occupation of Corregidor by American troops, and the eventual capture by the Japanese. Emphasis on American military strategy.*

Death March: The Survivors of Bataan, Donald Knox (1981). New York: Harcourt Brace Jovanovich. Oral history from 68 survivors of the Bataan Death March, with photos and maps.

Deliverance at Los Baños: The Dramatic True Story of Survival and Triumph in a Japanese Internment Camp, Anthony Arthur (1985). New York: St. Martin's Press. The rescue of 2,000 American civilians in Los Baños camp in the Philippines; told through diaries and interviews with the survivors.*

For You the War is Over: American Prisoners of War in Nazi Germany, David A. Foy (1984). New York: Stein and Day Publishers. Chronicle of the conditions endured by American POWs in German camps during World War II.*

The Knights of Bushido, Lord Russell (1958). New York: EP Dutton and Co. Chilling, minutely-detailed account of atrocities committed by the Japanese in World War II, including chapters on the prison camps and Japanese treatment of civilians. Closes with eyewitness reports on the postwar trials held in Tokyo by the United Nations.

Last Man Out, H. Robert Charles (1988). Austin, TX: Eakin Press. A survivor of the U.S.S. Houston, Charles describes his 43 months in slave labor camps in Burma and Saigon; also tells about Dr. Henri Hekking, the Dutch doctor who saved 250 American lives in the camps with herbal medicines.

The Longest Tunnel, Alan Burgess (1990). New York: Grove Weidenfeld Publishers. The story of 76 Allied POWs who tunneled out of a German Prison camp in the largest escape attempt of World War II.

The Other Nuremberg: The Untold Story of the Tokyo War Crimes Trials, Arnold C. Brackman (1987). New York: William Morrow and Company. Exhaustively researched account by an award-winning reporter who attended the trials and interviewed the infamous Tojo. Includes photos and transcripts, with a chapter on POWs.

Return to the Philippines, Rafael Steinberg (1980). Time-Life Books. Chronicles the recapture of the Philippine Islands by Allied troops; includes a chapter on the liberation of prison camps.

Scourge of the Swastika: A Short History of Nazi War Crimes, Lord Russell of Liverpool (1954). London: Cassell & Company. An eyewitness at the Nuremberg Trials, Russell provides official documentation of Nazi war crimes, as well as historical research and photos. Includes chapters on POWs, concentration camps and slave labor.

Surrender and Survival: The Experience of American POWs in the Pacific, 1941-1945, E. Bartlett Kerr (1985). New York: William Morrow and Company. Well-researched account of the treatment of American POWs in Japanese camps. Author's father died on the *Oryoku Maru*. Includes chapter on post-liberation.*

General

Prisoner of War, P.R. Reid (1984). New York: Beaufort Books. Entertaining, comprehensive record of POW experiences throughout recorded history. Includes photos and descriptions from wars throughout the world.

Prisoners of War, Ronald H. Bailey (1981). Alexandria, VA: Time-Life Books. Overview of POWs during the war and the conditions they endured. Includes sections on German prisoners held in America and the Soviet Union, as well as the camps run by the Germans and Japanese.

POW: Americans in Enemy Hands: World War II, Korea and Vietnam (1986). Arnold Shapiro Productions. Videocassette, 93 min. Shown first on national t.v.; recounts the loneliness, torture, and homecomings of nine POWs.*

Recovering from the War: A Woman's Guide to Helping Your Vietnam Vet, Your Family, and Yourself, Patience H.C. Mason (1990). New York: Penguin Books. Useful for the families of all veterans. Describes the stress of the war on those who stayed behind, and the difficulty of rebuilding relationships with the veteran. There is a lengthy chapter on PTSD, and an extensive bibliography catalogued by topic.

*Also available in the patients library at the Milwaukee VAMC:
one-to-five page descriptions of conditions in 74 Japanese and German camps, including names of prisoners and camp personnel, food, treatment, housing. Compiled from official records and the reports of ex-POWs, filed in a binder for easy photocopying.

Medical

The European Story, Stan Sommers (1980). Arlington, TX: National Medical Research Committee of the American Ex-Prisoners of War. Documents the plight of Allied prisoners of war in Europe, with emphasis on medical implications of their captivity.*

The Japanese Story, Stan Sommers (1980). Arlington, TX: National Medical Research Committee of the American Ex-Prisoners of War.

Documents the plight of Allied prisoners held by the Japanese, with emphasis on the medical implications of their captivity.*

The Korea Story, Stan Sommers (1981). Arlington, TX: National Medical Research Committee of the American Ex-Prisoners of War. American prisoners of the Koreans, their mistreatment, and subsequent medical complications.*

POW: Study of Former Prisoners of War (1980). Veterans Administra-0tion, Office of Planning and Program Evaluation (U.S. Printing Office No. 1980 0-625-455). Medical survey of former POWs from World War II, Korea, and Vietnam, with recommendations for providing them service.

Unit 731: Japan's Secret Biological Warfare in WWII, Peter Williams and David Wallace (1989). New York: The Free Press. Little-known medical experiments of Shiro Ishii, carried out on Russian, Chinese, American, British, and Australian prisoners of war. Ishii was never tried as a war criminal.

Fiction

A Gentle Occupation, Dirk Bogarde (1980). New York: Knopf.
A Hostage in Peking, Anthony Grey (1971). New York: Doubleday.
Andersonville, Mackinlay Kantor (1955). Cleveland:
        World Publishing Co.
The Bridge Over the River Kwai, Pierre Boulle (1954). New York:
        Vanguard Press.
Captain Caution, Kenneth Lewis Roberts (1934). New York:
        Doubleday.
The Case of Sergeant Grischa, Arnold Zweig (1929). New York:
        Grosset and Dunlap.
The Dirty Dozen, E.M. Nathanson (1965). New York: Random House.
Dog Tags, S. Becker (1973). New York: Random House.
Empire of the Sun, J.G. Ballard (1984). New York: Simon & Schuster.
King Rat, James Clavell (1983). New York: Delacorte Press.
The Last Mission, Harry Mazer (1979). New York: Delacorte Press.
The Legacy, Nevil Shute (1950). New York: Morrow.
The March, W.S. Kuniczak (1979). New York: Doubleday.
Schindler's List, Thomas Keneally (1982). New York: Simon & Schuster.
The Sea and Poison, Shusako Endo (1980). New York: Taplinger.
Slaughterhouse-Five, Kurt Vonnegut (1969). New York:
        Delacorte Press.
Some Kind of Hero, James Kirkwood (1975). New York: Crowell.
To the Ends of the Earth, Michael Talbot (1985). New York: Knopf.

The Valhalla Exchange, Henry Patterson (1976). New York:
Stein and Day.
Von Ryan's Express, David Westheimer (1964). New York:
Doubleday.
Wild Dogs of Chong Do, Clifford J. Stevens (1979). Huntington, IN:
Our Sunday Visitor.

Notes

Ex-Prisoners of War: Fact or Fiction? pp. 1 - 7

(1) From *The Retired Officer*, December 1985, p. 60. L.Colonel William R. Reitzell, AUS-Ret., from Worcester, Massachusetts, wrote: "I feel sorry for POWs but not to the extent of rewarding them with a medal. Surrender to the enemy and your country will award you a medal; keep fighting and it probably won't. Incredible!"

(2) This was true of World War II and Korean War veterans; however, POWs from the Vietnam and Persian Gulf Wars were awarded the Purple Heart in recognition of their POW status.

(3) Fifty years later, actual figures concerning the Bataan Death March vary widely, depending perhaps, on who's counting and whom they are counting. According to Eric Morris, in *Corregidor: End of the Line* (1988) New York: Stein and Day Publishers, 70,000 men started the march, and 54,000 reached Camp O'Donnell. Of 10,000 who died en route, of beatings, disease and execution, 2,330 are thought to have been Americans. Over the next six months, another 2,700 Americans and 29,000 Filipinos died at Camp O'Donnell. The high death rate was undoubtedly due, at least in part, to the brutal conditions of the Death March. (p.424)

On the other hand, in his 1992 statistical data on American prisoners of war, Charles Stenger reports that approximately 17,000 American nationals, and 12,000 Filipino scouts were captured in the Bataan-Corregidor combat zone. He estimates that 11,000 Americans and 4,000 Filipinos survived to the end of the war.

Historian Gregory Urwin of the University of Central Arkansas believes 66,000 Filipinos and up to 12,000 Americans were captured on Bataan alone.

Meanwhile, Elmer E. Long, National Secretary of the American Defenders of Bataan and Corregidor, has conducted a 20-year search of the National History Archives to determine the fate of American soldiers on a unit-by-unit basis. It is his conclusion that the records are so incomplete, and the March itself was so disorganized, that accurate numbers will never be known.

(4) The statistics of former POWs with post traumatic stress disorder vary according to any given study, but they are always much higher than for the general population. In a study of 188 World War II POWs, 66% had symptoms in their files one year after release that indicate

PTSD. Forty years later, 47% still had those symptoms, indicating the chronic nature PTSD can assume. From "Forty Year Follow-Up of United States Prisoners of War," by J.C. Kluznik, N. Speed, C. Van Valkenburg, et al., in *American Journal of Psychiatry* (1986) 143:1443-1445.

In another report, Raina E. Eberly and Brian E. Engdahl studied 426 former POWs in the Minneapolis VA region. They found 71% with a lifetime prevalence of PTSD, which they compared to .5% found in the general population. From "Prevalence of Somatic and Psychiatric Disorders Among Former Prisoners of War," in *Hospital and Community Psychiatry* (1991) 42:807-813.

(5) Both depression and uncontrollable emotional outbursts are common symptoms of post traumatic stress disorder. Other common symptoms are listed in Appendix 3 of this book, "Medical Effects of Incarceration." For a complete discussion of PTSD, and its effects on the veteran and family members, see *Recovering from the War*, by Patience H.C. Mason (1990). New York: Penguin Books.

(6) Alcoholism and disease are, perhaps, not-so-surprising results of a POW experience. The higher rate of suicide, homicide, and murder among former POWs is less commonly expected, although these findings are consistent among all POWs from World War II and the Korean War, and among Vietnam War combat veterans as a group. See: "A Follow-up Study of World War II Prisoners of War," by B.M. Cohen and M.Z. Cooper (1955). Washington DC: Veterans Administration Medical Monograph, USGPO, and "Follow-Up Studies of World War II and Korean War Prisoners: Study Plan and Mortality Findings," by M. Dean Nefzger in *American Journal of Epidemiology* (1970) 91:123-137, and "Follow-Up Studies of World War II and Korean War Prisoners: Morbidity, Disability and Maladjustments," by Gilbert W. Beebe in *American Journal of Epidemiology* (1975) 101:406-422, and "Follow-Up Studies of World War II and Korean Conflict Prisoners: Mortality to Jan. 1, 1976," by Robert J. Keehn in *American Journal of Epidemiology* (1980) 111:194-211.

These findings are also true of Australian ex-POWs: a survey from 1946 to 1963 found that more had died from suicide and motor vehicle accidents than did men in the general Australian population. Reported by Kerry J. Goulston, et al. in "Gastrointestinal Morbidity Among World War II Prisoners of War: 40 Years On," in *The Medical Journal of Australia* (1985) 143:6-10.

The statistics for Vietnam war combat veterans are extreme. According to a report in the *New England Journal of Medicine* (March 6, 1986), members of this group, which includes ex-POWs, are 65% more likely to die from suicide and 49% more likely to die in a motor vehicle accident than non-veterans the same age. In 1971, before the war had even ended, the National Council of Churches reported that 49,000 Vietnam veterans had died since returning from Vietnam. Another commonly cited statistic is that, by 1980, more Vietnam veterans had died of suicide than were killed during the war. From *Recovering from the War*, Patience H.C. Mason (1990). New York: Penguin Books, pp. 253, 302.

(7) For more information, read James Devereux's *The Story of Wake Island* (1947). New York: J.B. Lippincott Co. Colonel Devereux commanded the Marine garrison on Wake Island through 16 days of attack, then survived three years and 10 months as a prisoner of the Japanese.

(8) The decision not to equip Guam was made at least twice in the period preceding World War II. In a 1921 negotiation for naval power, America and Great Britain agreed not to build major bases in Hong Kong, Guam, or Manila in return for Japan's agreement to limit the use of military planes on certain islands. Then, in the summer of 1939, faced with a choice between defense of the Atlantic or the Pacific, America again decided to direct supplies and fire power from the Pacific Islands, in favor of the European theater. The decision was made by the U.S. Army and Navy Chiefs of Staff, who advised the president to resist defending the islands, even if Japan attacked. From *The Pacific War* by John Costello (1981). New York: Rawson, Wade Publishers Inc., pp. 38, 63-64.

(9) The 204 Marines stationed at Peking and Tientsin were among the first POWs of the war, surrendered by their commanding officers on December 8, 1942, without a shot fired. There was some hope initially that they might be quickly repatriated because of their status as "diplomatic personnel" in the two cities. Months passed, however, and no progress was made. The provision of the Boxer Protocol of 1901 under which they were to be repatriated turned out not to exist at all. In the end, the captured Marines were taken to the prison camps where they served out the war as POWs. From *Surrender and Survival* by E. Bartlett Kerr (1985). New York: William Morrow and Co., pp. 36-37.

(10) Accounts of Washington's "sacrifice" of the Philippines is reported in many books, including *Corregidor: End of the Line* by Eric Morris (1981). New York: Stein and Day Publishers.

(11) The fierce battle in the Ardennes – the Battle of the Bulge – involved a total of 600,000 American soldiers and 55,000 British. Nineteen thousand Americans were killed in battle, and 15,000 more were captured. According to Charles B. MacDonald, it is a misconception that American troops fled in disarray in the December, 1944, battle. "With the possible exception of the conglomerate group of infantrymen hurriedly thrown together . . . no front-line American unit fled without a fight." From *A Time for Trumpets: The Untold Story of the Battle of the Bulge* (1985). New York: Bantam Books, pp. 618-619.

(12) In every war, airmen have been at particular risk for capture by enemy forces. If they survive a crash landing or parachute escape, they

are likely to be injured when they reach the ground. In any event, they have little control over where they land; sometimes hostile civilians pose as great a danger as enemy troops. This situation is described by David A. Foy in *For You the War is Over: American Prisoners of War in Nazi Germany* (1984) New York: Stein and Day Publishers.

(13) According to studies published by the Veterans Administration, 41% of World War II European Theater POWs, 51% of World War II Pacific Theater POWs, and 59% of Korean War POWs were receiving service-connected disability compensation in 1980. There wasn't enough data on Vietnam POWs at the time to complete a survey. These figures are significant when compared to the non-POW veterans of each period: only 10% of all non-POW veterans of World War II, and 5% from the Korean War, were receiving compensation in 1980. Nevertheless, the figures are far lower than would seem justified by the conditions of imprisonment. Many doctors and former POWs believe *all* former POWs should receive service-connected disability compensation, not half of them. It is significant that, at the time of the study, one-fifth of World War II Pacific Theater POWs, one-fourth from the European Theater, and one-fourth of former Korean War POWs had never filed a claim for compensation. From *POW: Study of Former Prisoners of War* (1988). Veterans Administration, Office of Planning and Program Evaluation (U.S. Printing Office No. 1980 0-625-455), pp. 52, 61, 66, 82-83.

Anger and the Ex-POW pp. 11 - 15

(1) Every fall, people in the United States and in Japan hold memorial services for those who died in the atomic bombings of Hiroshima and Nagasaki. It is common to express anger at the United States for the civilian lives lost. What is not commonly known is that countless lives, both Allied and Japanese, were saved by ending the war so abruptly. It has been reported often that Japanese commanders issued orders to allow no one – Japanese or Allied, civilian or military – to be captured in the event of a land invasion of Japan. At the Tokyo War Crimes Trials, POW camp survivors testified they had been told by camp commandants they would be killed if Japan was invaded. A Japanese war diary found in a Formosa camp paraphrased the orders received by an adjutant of the 11th Military Police Unit on the island: "Whether [prisoners] are destroyed individually or in groups . . . dispose of them as the situation dictates. In any case, the object is not to allow the escape of a single one, to annihilate them all and to leave no trace." In light of such directives, and the obvious risks of a land invasion, the atomic bomb undoubtedly did save lives. From *The Knights of Bushido* by Lord Russell of Liverpool (1958). New York: EP Dutton & Co., pp. 115-116; and *The Other Nuremberg: The Untold Story of the Tokyo War Crimes Trials* by Arnold C. Brackman (1987). New York: William Morrow and Company, pp. 264-265.

(2) Post traumatic stress disorder did not become accepted as a diagnostic tool until the 1980s, when it was first applied to symptoms noted in returning Vietnam War veterans. Before this, similar symptoms were diagnosed as anxiety neurosis in World War II and Korean War veterans. According to a study of disability claims filed between 1946 and 1979, anxiety neurosis is the most common affliction diagnosed in former POWs of those two wars. The study also shows that the number of anxiety neurosis claims is sharply higher in former POWs than in non-prisoner veterans of the same wars, but fairly constant whether imprisonment was three months or less, or 25 months and more. For example, approximately 11% of World War II European Theater veterans were diagnosed with anxiety neurosis in the study period. However, 22-40% of former POWs in the European Theater carried the diagnosis, regardless of the length of their internment. From *POW: Study of Former Prisoners of War* (1988). Veterans Administration, Office of Planning and Program Evaluation (U.S. Printing Office No. 1980 0-625-455), pp. 83-83.

(3) From *The Thin Red Line* by James Jones (1962). New York: Charles Scribner's Sons.

(4) Shaky hands and tremulous voices are just two symptoms of anger. According to studies from as early as 1894, anger can produce reactions from twitching and sweating to choking, dizziness, headaches, and nausea. Other studies have shown that holding in thoughts or emotions requires physical effort and creates stress in the body. People who do this are prone to long-term health problems, or are at greater risk of eventual illness than people who express their anger. From *Anger: The Misunderstood Emotion* by Carol Tavris (1989). New York: Touchstone Books, pp. 70-71, 126.

(5) Many therapists hold to the idea that depression is anger turned inward. The theory was first postulated by Karl Abraham in 1911 and gained its footing under Sigmund Freud. However, in her book, *Anger: The Misunderstood Emotion* (1989, New York: Touchstone Books), Carol Tavris separates anger and depression, noting that each often exists without the other. Instead, she says, depression may be the sequel to anger, particularly if a person's wrath cannot be appeased. When anger does not restore a person's control over their environment, apathy and hopelessness may be the inevitable result. (pp. 107-108)

You Don't Look Disabled To Me pp. 19 - 24

(1) Drug use among former POWs is difficult to measure, but alcoholism seems to be higher than for the general population. In a study of 426 former POWs in the Minnesota VA Region, Raina E. Eberly and Brian E. Engdahl found a lifetime prevalence of alcohol abuse or de-

pendence in 21%.This compared in the study to 18% for the general population of American men aged 45 and older. Such studies, augmented by anecdotal information, lead one to believe that alcohol and drug abuse are common coping methods for former POWs. From "Prevalence of Somatic and Psychiatric Disorders Among Former Prisoners of War," in *Hospital and Community Psychiatry* (1991) 42:807-813.

(2) KZ Syndrome (konzentration slager) has also been called repatriation neurosis. Like post traumatic stress disorder, it may manifest immediately, or years after liberation. The primary symptoms are fatigue, difficulty concentrating, emotional instability and sleep disturbances. Many researchers have reported KZ not only in survivors of concentration camps, but also in persons who were in hiding or on the run from danger. Although KZ Syndrome is a distinct diagnosis from PTSD, the illnesses share many characteristics, and many ex-POWs could be reasonably diagnosed as having KZ Syndrome. For a complete list of diagnosed symptoms, see Appendix 3 in this book, " Medical Effects of Incarceration."

(3) Psychic numbing is extremely prevalent in former POWs, and is one of the symptoms of post traumatic stress disorder. In a study of 22 randomly selected Korean War POWs, Patricia Sutker, et al., found 18 (82%) reported feeling "emotionally numb". Only six (27%) of their matched counterparts in a group of Korean War combat veterans reported the same feelings. While psychic numbing robs the sufferer of emotional response, it is particularly difficult for the ex-POW's family to deal with. Spouses frequently report feeling an emotional wall in their relationships. From "Cognitive Deficits and Psychopathology Among Former Prisoners of War and Combat Veterans of the Korean Conflict," in *American Journal of Psychiatry* (1991) 148:67-72. It should be noted, too, that a feeling of numbness can also be a symptom of severe depression.

(4) Depression seems to be very prevalent in former POWs, as well as combat veterans, a theory confirmed both by study and by anecdotal evidence. In one survey of former POWs from World War II and the Korean War, between 37 and 57 percent had symptoms of depression. The normal rate for depressive symptoms in mid-age males was reported as 10%. By William Frank Page in "Summary Report of the 1984-85 Questionnaire Study of Former Prisoners of War and Combat Veterans," (1989) Washington DC: prepared for the Medical Follow-Up Agency of the Institute of Medicine, National Academy of Sciences.

Jim Goodwin, who worked with more than 300 Vietnam veterans in the Denver office of the Disabled American Veterans, wrote: "The vast majority of Vietnam combat veterans I have interviewed are depressed. Many have been continually depressed since their experiences in Vietnam . . . Many of these veterans have weapons in their possession, and they are no strangers to death . . . the possibility of suicide is always present. More Vietnam combat veterans have died since the war by their own hand than were actually killed in Vietnam." From "The Etiology of Combat-Related Post-Traumatic Stress Disorders," in *Post Traumatic Stress Disorders of the Vietnam Veteran*, Tom Williams, editor (1980). Cincinnati: Disabled American Veterans, p. 11.

(5) The roots of such fatigue could be organic, as in the brain changes, caused by malnutrition, that are suspected to be a root of KZ Syndrome. Increased fatigue is one of the most notable symptoms of KZ Syndrome. It should be noted that severe depression could also cause excessive fatigue. For a discussion of KZ Syndrome, see Appendix 3 of this book, "Medical Effects of Incarceration."

(6) The painful feet syndrome is a commonly-reported symptom of neuropathy and neuritis. The definition of neuritis is the inflammation of a nerve or its parts, and it is caused by Vitamin B deprivation, as well as by some infections, or by direct compression of the nerve. In a 1967 questionnaire study of 2,543 former POWs, Gilbert W. Beebe found that 71% of the World War II Pacific POWs had experienced painful feet in captivity; the figures for Korean War POWs and World War II European POWs were 57% and 36% respectively. From "Follow-Up Studies of World War II and Korean War Prisoners: Morbidity, Disability and Maladjustments," in *American Journal of Epidemiology* (1975) 101:406-422.

(7) Sleep disturbances are a common symptom of post traumatic stress disorder, and, according to at least one study, persist for decades after liberation from prison camp. In a survey of 426 former POWs in the Minneapolis VA region, Raina E. Eberly and Brian E. Engdahl found that 28% of the respondents experienced fitful, disturbed sleep and didn't feel rested most mornings. Thirty-six percent reported repetitive nightmares, while 24% experienced nightmares every few nights. From "Prevalence of Somatic and Psychiatric Disorders Among Former Prisoners of War," in *Hospital and Community Psychiatry* (1991) 42:807-813.

(8) No matter what the former POW's emotional condition, there is good reason to ask for help when filing a claim with the Veterans Administration. The VA itself can help, as can a qualified representative from a veterans group, usually called a service office. Stan Sommers makes the point emphatically in his booklet, *Claim Information* (1980). Arlington, TX: National Medical Research Committee of the American Ex-Prisoners of War. "The veteran or his survivors should *never* attempt to file a claim without seeking the assistance of a certified national service officer." (emphasis added) For more information on filing a claim, see Appendix 4 in this book, "Applying for Compensation and Benefits Through the Veterans Administration."

Disability Rating Problems for Ex-POWs pp. 27 - 35

(1) In a study of the compensation claims of former POWs from 1946 to 1979, the Veterans Administration reported the average degree of service-connected disability to be 27% for those in the European Theater of World War II, 40% for the Pacific Theater (29% for World War II POWs as a whole), and 36% for former Korean War POWs. These numbers are only slightly higher than the average disability ratings awarded non-POW veterans from World War II and the Korean War: 28% and 31% respectively. While the averages may have risen over the past decade, due to the implementation of the new protocol exams and more presumptive diseases, many former POWs and their advocates believe the disability ratings are still too low. From *POW: Study of Former Prisoners of War* (1988). Veterans Administration, Office of Planning and Program Evaluation (U.S. Printing Office No. 1980 0-625-455), p. 83.

For a discussion of the compensation rating system and application procedures, see Appendix 4 of this book, "Applying for Compensation and Benefits through the Veterans Administration."

(2) A study by the Veterans Administration in 1979 found that fewer than one-fifth of the former POWs from the European Theater in World War II who had filed a claim with the VA had repatriation medical records on file. The records for Pacific Theater POWs were better, with repatriation exams on file for three-fifths of those who had filed compensation claims. By the time of the Korean War, record keeping had improved so that all but 15% of former Korean War POWs had repatriation exams on file.

The VA has traditionally relied on repatriation medical exams and other service records when awarding compensation; however, even in cases where the records can be found, the information is often inadequate. In 1978, the Senate Committee on Veterans Affairs noted the deplorable state of repatriation medical records: "Because of the inadequate state of medical knowledge of various hardships suffered during internment . . . and because of the strong desire of former prisoners of war to return home as quickly as possible after World War II, those repatriation camps may have discharged veterans without thorough examinations and without close attention to their potential health problems. A major problem seems to be a lack of adequate records . . . Thus, 30 years later, a former POW suffering from a debilitating disease that may have resulted from his or her internment, may encounter extreme difficulty in proving service-connection." From *POW: Study of Former Prisoners of War* (1988). Veterans Administration, Office of Planning and Program Evaluation (U.S. Printing Office No. 1980 0-625-455), pp. 45, 52, 61, 66.

(3) Actually, the Department of Veterans Affairs places the burden of proof on the claimant – if a former POW cannot prove that a disability has its origin in the prison camp experience, the VA generally feels no obligation to pay compensation. The exception to this rule is presumptive disease, explained in the next note. For a discussion of compensation claims denied, see: *American Ex-Prisoners of War: A Modern Day Tragedy*, Stan Sommers (1980). Arlington, TX: National Medical Research Committee of the American Ex-Prisoners of War.

(4) Presumptive conditions are those the Department of Veterans Affairs considers to be service-connected, regardless of any lack of evidence tendered by the claimant. Currently, there are 11 categories of presumptive conditions. For the complete list, turn to Appendix 4 in this book, "Applying for Compensation Benefits through the Veterans Administration."

(5) As of 1980, approximately one-fifth of World War II Pacific Theater POWs, and one-fourth of World War II European Theater and Korean War POWs, had never filed a claim for compensation with the Veterans Administration. From *POW: Study of Former Prisoners of War* (1988). Veterans Administration, Office of Planning and Program Evaluation (U.S. Printing Office No. 1980 0-625-455), pp. 52, 61, 66.

(6) For a more complete account, see "The Oryoku Maru," in Appendix 1 of this book, "What It Was Like: Prison Camp Experiences as Told by the Survivors."

(7) In a study encompassing more than 19,000 veterans from 1946 to 1965, M. Dean Nefgzer found that former POWs died from accidents, suicide and murder far more often than their non-POW veteran counterparts. Such deaths were particularly high for Pacific Theater and Korean War POWs, especially in the two years immediately following liberation. From "Follow-Up Studies of World War II and Korean War Prisoners: Study Plan and Mortality Findings," in *American Journal of Epidemiology* (1970) 91:123-137.

(8) In addition to the former POWs who have managed to keep working over the years, there is a significant number who have dropped out of the workforce because of their disability. According to a Veterans Administration survey of its files for the years 1946-1979, five percent of European Theater POWs from World War II, and 22% from the Pacific Theater were deemed unemployable by dint of their disabilities. For Korean War POWs, the figure was nine percent. From *POW: Study of Former Prisoners of War* (1988). Veterans Administration, Office of Planning and Program Evaluation (U.S. Printing Office No. 1980 0-625-455), p. 90.

Those who work also have a difficult time. In a survey of 257 of his ex-POW patients, Dr. Murray Bernstein of the Zablocki Medical Center in Milwaukee found these statistics: 71% completed high school, while only 6% completed higher education. Twenty percent have abused alcohol for periods of up to one year since their return. And, while 98% reported they were employed within two months of their release, 83% also reported they moved from job to job for the first three years. Twenty-three percent of these men reported themselves to have obsessive working patterns. From a speech given at a conference, April 12, 1986, audience unknown.

(9) Currently, Canada seems to be the only nation which provides a standard disability rating to all former POWs. It is a tiered system, with former prisoners of the Japanese who were held 12 months or more receiving 50% compensation. Those held fewer than 12 months receive 20%, those held by other powers up to 18 months receive 10%. If a former POW was held 18-30 months they receive 15%, and if they were held more than 30 months by powers other than Japan, they receive 20% standard compensation. From *POW: Study of Former Prisoners of War* (1988). Veterans Administration, Office of Planning and Program Evaluation (U.S. Printing Office No. 1980 0-625-455), pp. 130-131.

The United States does have a law, instituted in 1986, providing per diem payments to service members and federal civilians who are held hostage or taken prisoner of war. In the case of Persian Gulf POWs, the per diem paid was supposed to be $133 for each day of captivity; however, a little-known 1987 amendment to the law would cut that amount by 50%. In either case, this is a lump sum payment and not based on disability or the long-term effects of captivity.

I Survived, But Was It Worth It? pp. 39 - 41

(1) Every period of war has brought enormous changes to the homefront, in everything from economy and productivity to entertainment and cultural values. For instance, an American soldier returning in early 1946 from three years in a Japanese prison camp came home to 3.5 million women in the workforce (wearing trousers of all things), a nationwide housing shortage, and daylight savings time. They learned of Franklin Roosevelt's death, Shirley Temple's marriage, the cancellation of "Amos and Andy", and the rising popularity of someone named Frank Sinatra. Some changes are easy to assimilate, but others – particularly in family roles and relationships – can cause years of confusion and even trauma.

A Wife's View of Her Ex-POW Mate pp. 45 -50

(1) This happened to some of the women participating in Dr. Keln-hofer's spouse support group in Seattle, Washington, in the 1980s. In her book *Recovering from the War* (1990, New York: Penguin Books), Patience H.C. Mason describes her own PTSD symptoms from living with a Vietnam veteran. She experienced isolation, rage, buried anger, headaches and neck and back pain, distrust of others, hyperalertness, depression, and suicidal feelings. In one passage she describes trying to kill her husband and wanting to kill herself before she sought help through therapy. (pp. 270-271)

(2) In *Recovering From the War*, Patience H.C. Mason notes: "Getting a guy with PTSD to talk is almost impossible." She breaks down PTSD sufferers into two broad categories, which she calls denial and intru-sion. Those in the denial category work to suppress their memories and push the experiences to the back of their mind. Those in the intru-sion category can't stop thinking or talking or dreaming about the ex-periences. Obviously, these are generalizations, but helpful nonethe-less for someone living with a person who has PTSD. (1990, New York: Penguin Books), pp. 262-263.

(3) Although marriage statistics for ex-POWs are hard to come by, there is reason to believe these relationships are under more stress than the average union. In a survey of 257 of his own ex-POW patients at the Zablocki Medical Center in Milwaukee, Dr. Murray Bernstein found that, while 92% were married, 85% reported communication difficul-ties with their partners. Seventy-six percent of the wives in these marriages said they felt an emotional wall between themselves and their mates. (Reported by Dr. Bernstein at a conference, April 12, 1986, audience unknown).

Also, it is noteworthy that 38% of the marriages of Vietnam veterans ended within six months of their return from Southeast Asia (*Mental Health Problems of Vietnam Era Veterans*, President's Commission on Mental Health (1978). Washington DC: U.S. Government Printing Office, 3:1321-1328), and that the divorce rate for Vietnam veterans is higher than for the general population (*The Adjustment of Vietnam Era Veterans to Civilian Life* (1979). New York: Center for Policy Research). It is perhaps not coincidental that a very high number of Vietnam veterans have been diagnosed with post traumatic stress disorder. From "The 'Veteran System' With a Focus on Women Partners," in *Post Traumatic Stress Disorders of the Vietnam Veteran*, Tom Williams, editor (1980). Cincinnati: Disabled American Veterans, p 100.

(4) Among the benefits a woman might expect from a support group for spouses of ex-POWs: raised self-esteem, increased problem-solv-ing skills, identification of needs, self-awareness, healthier relation-ship with her husband, and new friends who understand her situation.

On the other hand, Candis M. Williams warns against expecting too much: the focus should be on helping the woman, not on solving all her husband's problems. "If the women can derive some security and strength from each other, they will be better equipped to help their mates and enhance their relationships. But let us not place these women in the impossible position of being 'therapists' for their partners." From "The 'Veteran System' With a Focus on Women Partners," in *Post Traumatic Stress Disorders of the Vietnam Veteran*, Tom Williams, editor (1980). Cincinnati: Disabled American Veterans, pp. 94-95, 113-115.

(5) For more suggestions on effecting change in the legislature, in the DVA, and in the lives of ex-POWs and their families, see Appendix 6 of this book, "Recommendations to Help Ex-POWs."

Group Therapy and The Ex-POW pp. 53 - 54

(1) Another benefit of speaking out may be improved health. In 1987-88, psychologist James Pennebaker studied a group of Holocaust survivors who had never spoken about their concentration camp experiences – although they thought about the camps constantly. Pennebaker asked some subjects to talk about those experiences, either to a tape recorder or an anonymous listener. When he tracked the subjects 14 months later, he found a surprising link between "confession" and improved health. The more each person revealed in the experiment, the fewer their illnesses and trips to the doctor in the subsequent 14 months. Pennebaker's theory is that talking or writing about the trauma forces a person to organize and gain control over their thoughts, and gives structure to the event. Otherwise, the memories exhibit themselves as "vague, fragmented images, nightmarish glimpses of the trauma." From *Anger: The Misunderstood Emotion*, by Carol Tavris (1989). New York: Touchstone Books, pp. 156-157.

APPENDIX 2: Questioning Japan's Honor pp. 99 - 104

(1) Even the apologies tendered to other countries are somewhat backhanded; Japan has not yet admitted to being an aggressor, but only to being contrite. Japanese Prime Minister Toshiki Kaifu told 800 Chinese people gathered in a Beijing hall in August 1991: "With our sense of sincere contrition at the past war we have truly been reborn as a nation for peace. The Japanese people are determined never again to make war," and "There was an unfortunate period, for which Japan should deeply reproach itself, in the long history of friendship between Japan and China." (reported in the *Beijing Review*, August 1991, 34:33, p. 7) In May of 1991, Kaifu made an apology directly to Canadian Prime Minister Brian Mulroney, who later said that Kaifu expressed

"sadness and contrition". In May 1991 presss releases, the War Amputations of Canada called the statement "hollow" because it avoided the issue of compensation for the slave labor of POWs.

Japanese Prime Minister Kiichi Miyazawa did apologize in January 1992 to Korean women used as "comfort women" – literally sex slaves – during Japan's occupation of Korea, from 1910 to 1945. The apology was forced by a month of public demonstrations in Seoul, preceding Miyazawa's diplomatic visit there. (*Ms.*, March / April 1992, 2:5, p.11)

Despite such gestures, however, ill will still exists toward Japan. Hidejiro Kotani, columnist and emeritus president of the Himeji Gakuin Women's Junior College in Japan, writes that the hatred of North Koreans for Japan will have a significant effect on the recent efforts of those countries to normalize relations. Similar negotiations with South Korea took 14 years to finalize. (*Business JAPAN*, November 1991, 36:11, p.7)

It should be noted that at least one citizen group has begun to exert pressure on the Japanese government to provide adequate apologies. In November, 1991, Daizaburo Yui wrote to Canadian ex-POW groups expressing remorse for Japan's actions in the war, and a promise to pressure the government to apologize and give compensation to former POWs. Yui is a professor of contemporary history at Hitotsubashi University in Tokyo, and executive director of the recently-formed group, Concerned Japanese Citizens on the 50th Anniversary of the Outbreak of the Asian Pacific War. From *The Little WigWag*, newsletter of the Survivors of Wake, Guam and Cavite, February, 1992, p.3.

(2) Reported by the Associated Press, December 30, 1988. Nagasaki Mayor Hitoshi Motoshima said "I believe the emperor shares responsibility for the war, as well as all of us who lived in that period." Motoshima was then besieged by death threats and several days of public demonstrations, before suffering a gunshot wound in an assassination attempt.

(3) The Greater East Asia Co-Prosperity Sphere was problematic from its inception, around 1939. The idea was something akin to the current European Community (EC) with one exception: Japan would be the nucleus and main beneficiary of the partnership with other Asian countries, which included Malaya, Indonesia and the Philippines. The outbreak of war complicated the program and led to its ultimate ruin. In desperate need of raw materials, Japan simply confiscated what it required from the surrounding countries, effectively co-opting the original promise of economic harmony. By the war's end, damage to the local economies and communication structures combined with a rise in nationalist movements to bring an end to the remnants of the Co-Prosperity Sphere. From *The Rise of Modern Japan*, W.G. Beasley

(1990). New York: St. Martin's Press, pp. 204-208.

(4) Personal honor is exceptionally important to the Japanese. According to John Randle and Mariko Watanabe, authors of *Coping with Japan* (1985) New York: Basil Blackwell, "It is true that suicides still tend to occur over matters of shame – accumulating debts or disgrace at work, and even today a member of a work group might commit suicide to exonerate his group." If this happens, his company might make a cash payment to the family, which they don't do if the worker merely resigns. The authors note, however, that suicide as a method of preserving honor has lost popularity since World War II, when tens of thousands of Japanese killed themselves rather than surrender to the Allies. (p. 147)

(5) Obviously not all Japanese hold respect for Japan's war criminals; probably only a minority do. But enough instances come to mind to indicate the criminals are not wholly despised either. Many point to the fact that Emperor Hirohito was never prosecuted for his part in the war, and that he held his position as Japan's figurehead until his death in 1989. A more telling example is related by Arnold C. Brackman in *The Other Nuremberg: The Untold Story of the Tokyo War Crimes Trials* (1987, New York: William Morrow and Company, pp. 27-28). In 1978, 14 war criminals, including Premier Hideki Tojo, Japan's Minister of War from 1940-1944 who was executed for war atrocities, were given high honor. They were enshrined as martyrs at the Yasukuni Shrine, Japan's most revered Shinto temple. The high priests said the enshrinement was justified because the men had "devoted their lives to the Emperor and to Japan." Many Japanese did not agree, and the Japanese press was critical of the decision. Nevertheless, Premier Masayoshi Ohira visited the shrine and paid respects to the war dead, including the convicted criminals – an act which is still remembered with distaste by many.

(6) Although the initial death count for the Rape of Nanking was 42,000, further evidence has raised it to 100,000 at the minimum and 300,000 at the maximum. Reported by Michael Browning of the *Miami Herald*, December 27, 1987 ("Chinese vent anger at Japan for 'Rape of Nanking'").

(7) Reported by the Associated Press, June 12, 1988. Okuno was forced to resign from his post after making statements such as this one: "[Japan] fought to protect itself at a time when the white race had turned Asia into a colony." His view was supported by 41 of the 445 parliamentarians of the governing Liberal Democratic Party.

(8) Reported by the Associated Press, June 12, 1988. Fujio was fired from his position for this stand, because of the immediate protests raised by South and North Korea.

(9) Reported in the *Japan Times*, October 4, 1989 ("Court upholds screening of academic textbooks"). The court ruling stemmed from a 1980 lawsuit brought by history professor Saburo Ienaga against the Education of Ministry. It was Ienaga's third suit, claiming a violation of his freedom of expression and academic freedom. The court ruled against Ienaga in almost every instance.

(10) Reported by the Associated Press, June 12, 1988. The Education Ministry, bowing to pressure from China and South Korea, later promised to amend some passages.

(11) Reported by the *New York Times*, January 22, 1988 ("Atrocities cut from 'Emperor' for movie's showing in Japan") and the Associated Press, June 12, 1988. The Japanese distributor actually did delete footage which depicted Japanese soldiers killing Chinese civilians and dumping their bodies in a pit. The footage was eventually restored. In another incident, Japanese theaters refused to show the comedy "Gung Ho" because of objections raised by the Nissan auto company.

(12) Racist behavior in Japan is one of that nation's continuing public relations problems. In a country with a one percent minority population, there is little impetus for affirmative action or mass education on minority issues. In his book, *The Japanese Mind*, Robert C. Christopher notes that the problem extends to foreigners as well: "Something that few if any Japanese are prepared to admit is that along with defensiveness, their exclusionary behavior also rests on a strongly entrenched superiority complex," and "The more eagerly and knowledgeably a foreigner seeks assimilation into Japanese society, the more firmly that society rejects him." (1983, New York: Simon and Schuster, p. 186)

As for being a chosen people, in fact, Japanese folklore does maintain that the Japanese descended from heaven, and that the first emperor was the great-great-grandson of the sun goddess. Despite the "divine" origin of the emperor, however, modern Japanese probably derive more of their pride from a sense of economic or cultural superiority, than from connection to their singularly impersonal royal family. From *The Insider's Guide to Japan* by Peter Popham (1987). New Jersey: Hunter Publishing Inc., pp. 14-15.

(13) Internationally, distrust still stems from Japan's economic abuse of the Co-Prosperity Sphere, and from that country's aggressive behavior during World War II. According to Robert Christopher in *The Japanese Mind*, Asia views Japan as ". . . suspect outsiders. The Chinese . . .tend to consider the Japanese crude and unsophisticated. . .the South Koreans. . . bitterly dislike the Japanese and are determined to make them atone indefinitely for the 35 years during which Korea was part of the Japanese Empire," and "As for the Southeast Asians, they have their own unhappy memories. . . and in any case do not for the most part find the Japanese socially or culturally compatible." (pp. 176-177)

(14) Accurate records on POW labor are difficult to come by. According to a report prepared by a professor of Japan's National Defense Academy, 55,000 POWs were used on the Thai-Burma Railway alone. Given the source, these figures are apt to be low. Other sources, such as Brackman's *The Other Nuremberg*, add 250,000 local civilian internees to that project. The Defense Academy's report notes a number of industries which benefited from POW labor, including engineering, construction, iron and steel manufacturing, mining, shipbuilding, transportation, and "other manufacturing industries." From "Unprepared Regrettable Events: A Brief History of Japanese Practices on Treatment of Allied War Victims During the Second World War," by Sumio Adachi of Yokosuka City, National Defense Academy. Date unknown: post-1983.

Guy J. Kelnhofer, Jr., Ph.D.

Guy J. Kelnhofer, Jr., a native of Manitowoc, Wisconsin, served in the United States Marine Corps from 1939 until his honorable discharge in 1946 at the age of 24. Dr. Kelnhofer spent most of his service time in the South Pacific, and was on Wake Island when he was captured by the Japanese in 1941. For the next three years and ten months, he was held in prison camps in China, Korea, and Japan. When Japan surrendered in 1945, he was a slave laborer in the coal mines of Hokkaido. Upon his release, Dr. Kelnhofer was awarded a 50% medical disability rating, later upgraded to 100%, for his service-connected injuries. His many service awards include a Purple Heart, the Presidential Unit Citation and the Prisoner of War medal.

After his discharge, Dr. Kelnhofer enrolled at the University of Chicago on the GI Bill. There he met Maria, then a nursing student, and they were married in 1948. Together they raised three children. Dr. Kelnhofer went on to earn his Ph.D. in resources planning. He and Maria have worked in several countries and in many regions of the United States. Guy's many positions have included: section leader for the Puerto Rico Planning Board; chief area planner of the Tennessee State Planning Commission; director of water resources planning and director of community planning, both for the State of Minnesota; professor at Georgia Institute of Technology in Atlanta; private planning consultant; project director with the United Nations; regional planner in Venezuela for the Joint Center for Urban Studies at Harvard University and the Massachusetts Institute of Technology; and research director for the National Waterway Conference, Incorporated.

Maria Kelnhofer became a licensed physician and has studied and practiced medicine throughout the United States and in Romania. In addition to her medical degree, one year of residency in ophthalmology, and four years of residency in psychiatry, she has completed a master's degree in public health, and has met all the requirements except the dissertation for a doctorate in psychology. She has also served one-year fellowships both in ophthalmic pathology and in geriatric psychiatry. Today, Dr. Kelnhofer continues her private psychiatry practice in the Minneapolis/St. Paul area.

Guy Kelnhofer retired in 1983, suffering the effects of severe hearing loss, chronic vertigo, and post traumatic stress disorder. He has been active in therapy groups for ex-POWs, and has spoken often on the effects of prison camp experiences on the lives of ex-POWs. Maria Kelnhofer also has been active in issues affecting ex-POWs, and is known nationally for the workshops she has presented to the spouses of former prisoners of war.

The Kelnhofers currently reside in a suburb of Minneapolis.

Amy Lindgren

Amy Lindgren is a professional writer and editor based in St. Paul, Minnesota. She holds a bachelor's degree in English from The College of St. Catherine. The author of hundreds of published articles, Ms. Lindgren writes often about such diverse topics as law, employment, feminism, and health. She is also the founder and owner of a vocational counseling service, ProtoType Career Services, which specializes in helping people in transition. Ms. Lindgren is currently writing *Surviving a Layoff: Prospering in a Time of Change*, due for publication in 1993.

Comments?

We'd like to know what you think of *Understanding the Former Prisoner of War: Life after Liberation*. Are you a former prisoner of war? Do you live or work with someone who is? Do you provide services for ex-POWs?

Please tell us your reactions to this book, or a little bit about yourself. All comments will be forwarded to the author, Guy Kelnhofer, Jr.

Please send comments to:

> Banfil Street Press
> 244 Banfil Street
> St. Paul, MN 55102

Book Order Form

To order more copies of *Understanding the Former Prisoner of War: Life after Liberation* please mail a check or money order with this form to:

Banfil Street Press, 244 Banfil Street, St. Paul, MN 55102

Name _____

Address _____

City _____ State _____ Zip _____

      Hardcover with dust jacket _____ (quantity) x $29.95 _____

      Soft cover edition _____ (quantity) x $19.95 _____

      Please add 6.5% sales tax in Minnesota. _____

      Shipping: $2.50 for first book, $1.00 for
             each additional book. _____

Total enclosed: (# of books + shipping + tax if applicable) $ _____

Is this book intended as a gift? If so, please include recipient's name and address for direct delivery:

Name _____

Address _____

City _____ State _____ Zip _____

Book Order Form

To order more copies of *Understanding the Former Prisoner of War: Life after Liberation* please mail a check or money order with this form to:

Banfil Street Press, 244 Banfil Street, St. Paul, MN 55102

Name _____

Address _____

City _____ State _____ Zip _____

      Hardcover with dust jacket _____ (quantity) x $29.95 _____

      Soft cover edition _____ (quantity) x $19.95 _____

      Please add 6.5% sales tax in Minnesota. _____

      Shipping: $2.50 for first book, $1.00 for
             each additional book. _____

Total enclosed: (# of books + shipping + tax if applicable) $ _____

Is this book intended as a gift? If so, please include recipient's name and address for direct delivery:

Name _____

Address _____

City _____ State _____ Zip _____